I ho[pe] ... [help] ... [es]t. of Kathy I loved her Debbie mill

DAILY WORD for HEALING

BLESSING YOUR LIFE WITH MESSAGES OF HOPE AND RENEWAL

Written and edited by Colleen Zuck,
Janie Wright, and Elaine Meyer

B

BERKLEY BOOKS, NEW YORK

B

A Berkley Book
Published by The Berkley Publishing Group
A division of Penguin Putnam Inc.
375 Hudson Street
New York, New York 10014

PRINTING HISTORY
Daybreak Books hardcover edition published in 2000
Berkley trade paperback edition / November 2001

Visit our website at
www.penguinputnam.com

Library of Congress Cataloging-in-Publication Data

Zuck, Colleen,
    Daily word for healing : blessing your life with messages of hope and
    renewal / written and edited by Colleen Zuck, Janie Wright, and Elaine
    Meyer.
        p.   cm.
    Originally published: Emmaus, Pa.: Daybreak Books, 2000.
    ISBN 0-425-18171-5
        1. Devotional calendars.   2. Spiritual healing.   I. Wright, Janie.
    II. Meyer, Elaine.   III. Title.

    BV4810.Z82   2001
    242'.2—dc21   2001035259

PRINTED IN THE UNITED STATES OF AMERICA

10   9   8   7   6   5   4   3   2   1

An Invitation

Daily Word is the magazine of Silent Unity, a worldwide prayer ministry now in its second century of service. Silent Unity believes that:

◆ *All people are sacred*
◆ *God is present in all situations*
◆ *Everyone is worthy of love, peace, health, and prosperity*

Silent Unity prays with all who ask for prayer. Every prayer request is held in absolute confidence, and there is never a charge. You are invited to contact Silent Unity 24 hours a day, any day of the year.

Write: Silent Unity, 1901 NW Blue Parkway
Unity Village, MO 64065-0001
Or call: (816) 969-2000   Fax: (816) 251-3554
www.unityworldhq.org

There's More!

If you enjoy these inspirational messages, you may wish to subscribe to *Daily Word* magazine and receive a fresh, contemporary, uplifting message for each day of the month. With its inclusive, universal language, this pocket-size magazine is a friend to millions of people around the world.

For a free sample copy or for subscription information regarding *Daily Word* in English (regular and large-type editions) or in Spanish, please write:

Silent Unity, 1901 NW Blue Parkway
Unity Village, MO 64065-0001
Or call: (800) 669-0282   Fax: (816) 251-3554
www.unityworldhq.org

List of Articles

INTRODUCTION

P erhaps what you need more than anything is to know there is hope—hope for a healthier, more fulfilling life for you and your loved ones.

Then allow yourself to believe that you and your loved ones will never need to face a healing challenge alone. This is true, for the spirit of God that breathed the breath of life into you continues to breathe through you. Every life-affirming thought you think and word of healing you speak call for the life of God within to live out through you as healing and renewal.

The material in this book is from *Daily Word*, the monthly magazine of inspiration and prayer support from the Silent Unity prayer ministry. Silent Unity has been praying with people for over 100 years. Many people whom we have prayed with over the years have told us that prayer is one of the most powerful healing resources that they have applied in their own lives and have offered in loving support of others.

We can all make a sacred investment in the healing and health of each other through prayer. Any one person's healing need touches the lives of many: family, friends, coworkers, doctors, nurses, and other health care workers.

How to Use This Book

This book has been written and compiled to help everyone who is seeking greater health, experiencing a healing challenge, or helping others in need of healing. As you read day by day, page by page, we trust that you will come to know that these messages of life and healing were written especially for you, for they are about and for the child of God that each one of us is. We are God's creations of magnificent design, for healing has been imprinted within our very cells. We have been created to heal. So begin right now to claim a healing, whether it is for your body, your mind, your finances, or your relationships.

1. **Articles:** In his story, "Yes, God Is Listening," Bill Goss describes that hearing a diagnosis of cancer was like hearing "You are alone." Against all odds, Bill lived and has been cancer-free for more than 5 years. He explains how building a strong faith will build a strong immune system.

Each story—from the one about the man who received a new heart to the amputee skier who won an Olympic medal—is rich with hope and inspiration, reminders that no one is ever alone in any challenge.

2. **Daily messages:** You may choose to start with the first message, "Healing Life" and read straight through to the last message, "God Is My All." Or you may wish to search through the themes of the daily messages and choose a message that speaks directly to a challenge you are facing. Life-affirming words call forth a healing response.

3. **Meditation, Prayer, and Beloved Pages:** You will discover this series in a three-page format at intervals throughout the book. You will move from a guided meditation—an exercise in relaxation and inner reflection—to a prayer that prepares you to come fully into the presence of God and listen. Next in the series is a "Beloved" message, based on the principles of a loving, ever-present Creator, that is an invitation to experience the presence of God.

You are a unique child of God, and it is an honor to share the inspiration and prayers of Silent Unity with you.

A NEW LIFE
BY MICK DUSTIN

I received the gift of life twice—once at birth and then again through a heart transplant. Just before I was to undergo surgery, the surgeon and all who would be assisting him gathered around me. We held hands, and I said the "Prayer for Protection" for them and for me. I affirmed that God was working through their hands and that the prayers of everyone who was praying for me would be supporting them throughout the surgery. All was peaceful, and the last thing I remember before I went to sleep was saying "Amen."

When the surgeon came into my room the next day, I didn't recognize him at first. I looked at him and rather questioningly said, "I know you." He said, "Yes, we prayed together last night."

During the 2 years and 4 months prior to the transplant, I had been in and out of the hospital several times. I had experienced two heart attacks, angioplasty, and a five-way bypass surgery. I lost 120 pounds, and my heart was functioning at only 20 percent capacity.

There was no question that the second heart attack was stronger and harder than the first. After bypass surgery, I had only enough strength to walk from one room to another. Then I had to rest.

Coughing is a normal part of recovery for a heart patient; it clears the lungs. I was coughing so hard, however, that three of the wire sutures holding my sternum together broke, and the sternum did not heal. So I was in constant pain.

One day I fell in the driveway of our home after letting our dog out for a run. I wasn't able to get back up, so I just sat there until I regained enough strength to pull myself up.

When I went back for a checkup, my doctors suggested that I consider being evaluated for a heart transplant. They gave me a list of several hospitals that specialized in this procedure, and I chose one in St. Louis, several hundred miles away from home on the opposite side of the state.

Christine, my wife, spent that Christmas and New Year's season with me in ICU as I was going through tests in the hospital in St. Louis. The doctors determined that I was a good candidate for a heart transplant and sent me home to wait. Six weeks later I was back in our local hospital with pneumonia, which was complicated by a case of the hiccups that lasted 9 days. After the pneumonia, I was in and out of the St. Louis hospital several more times while awaiting my transplant.

Through it all, I kept repeating this affirmation: "*I am in God, and God is in me.*" I prayed this affirmation over and over again, realizing that my will and God's will were one. But I also kept repeating something else: "Whenever

I seem to be moving in the right direction—toward healing—I get snakebit; something unexpected happens, and I'm back in the hospital. I just don't understand!"

Christine said, "Honey, you might just want to take a look at your statement about being snakebit and come up with a new affirmation." When she said the word *affirmation*, I realized I had been cancelling my life-affirming affirmation with this negative one.

Then I began listening to what I was really saying. That evening I started singing the song "I'm Ready for a Miracle," and my attitude took a positive shift. I was ready for a miracle and, therefore, a miracle happened. The right heart, the more-than-perfect heart for me, was available within a couple of weeks.

During the 2 years when my heart was failing, my other organs had to take up the slack. My lungs had filled with fluid, and I had a hard time breathing. Within minutes of regaining consciousness from the heart-transplant surgery, I could tell that my lungs were stronger. My precious new heart was not only functioning, it had already taken on the added responsibility that my lungs and other organs had been struggling with. I took my first deep breath in months and realized that my lungs had already begun to clear.

That was in July. I was back home during the first part of October and able to lead a Silent Unity prayer service at Unity Village, where I had discovered my own spiritual roots and become a Unity minister. I had been blessed by this incredible, dynamic connection with the people who were praying for me. Now I was in the Silent Unity Chapel praying for others. I didn't have to know them or what they were going through to pray effectively. I affirmed for them what I had affirmed for myself: "*You are in God, and God is in you.*"

Throughout my journey toward healing, I knew that people were praying for me. At times I felt waves of prayer washing over me. Christine was always there for me, my mother came to stay with me in St. Louis, and my sister did research about heart transplants, sharing information with many other people to encourage them to sign donor cards. My brother told me that the *Daily Word* message on the day I received my new heart was written especially for me.

Silent Unity prayed for me. Friends from around the world prayed for me and sent me cards and letters. I felt a peace that I can best describe as the absolute calm in the eye of the storm. I was able to stay centered in the presence of God in the midst of all that was going on around me. My whole body responded to life-affirming prayer.

My recovery has gone extremely well, and I have gained new strength. What will I choose to do with my new gift of life? I don't know just yet, but I do know that it will be whatever pulls me forward and helps me to continue to realize that God is in me and I am in God, that I am alive with the life of God.

Healing Life

—— ◆ ——

God, the source of all life and healing,
is healing me now!

I give thanks for all the people who assist in helping me
and others to heal; however, I know and acknowledge
that God is the source of all healing.

God is the very life that animates me, filling every
cell of my body with the energy and ability to function.
God is the master creator of life, and it is God who
makes me whole and well.

From the top of my head to the tips of my toes, I am
energized by the life of God. I am strengthened and
renewed with life so that I am vibrantly alive!

Regardless of appearances, divine life is mightier than
any sickness or disease. With God as my source of
healing, I can overcome any challenge to my well-being.

Yes, God is healing me now! I am grateful for the
presence of God within—my constant, unfailing
connection to the source of all life in the universe.

"I am the Lord who heals you."
—Exodus 15:26

Faith

——◆——

My faith in God is a silent, powerful prayer.

In the quiet of prayer, I am totally in the presence of God. Breathing deeply and evenly, I give my complete attention to God, and a revitalization takes place within me. My faith, as well as my body, is strengthened.

Prayer is a faith builder, and daily prayer is the spiritual foundation of my life. Prayer and faith support and enhance each other. So when I need more faith, I know to pray. In those times when I don't know how or what to pray, I let my faith be a powerful silent prayer.

God answers my every prayer, and my faith helps me recognize the answers that I might otherwise miss. Faith listens and perceives the language of Spirit. I understand that the answer to every prayer is a confirmation of God's love for me.

> "On the day I called, you answered me,
> you increased my strength of soul."
> —Psalms 138:3

Caregiver

—◆—

*I care about and for the family
of God in loving ways.*

In one of Jesus' teachings, He proclaimed the
importance of caregivers. He told of a king who said to
those who had fed, clothed, and cared for others, "Truly
I tell you, just as you did it to one of the least of these
who are members of my family, you did it to me"
(Matthew 25:40).

The care that one member of the family of God gives
to another member surely honors God. Every person in
the world can be a caregiver because caregivers are
simply giving from the spirit of God within them.

Sometimes that care includes feeding and clothing
children or adults who cannot care for themselves.
Other times it is giving an encouraging word or a hug.
Caregivers let the love of God within be expressed as
caring words and actions.

> "I was hungry and you gave me food, I was thirsty
> and you gave me something to drink,
> I was a stranger and you welcomed me."
> —Matthew 25:35

Grace

— ◆ —

*The grace of God is my
continual, eternal support.*

If someone were to ask me what God's grace means to me, I might find it difficult to describe. I do know the glory of divine grace and how completely it blesses me.

God's grace is so encompassing that all I could ever need or desire is available to me. Through grace, the love of God in action, I am encouraged to live life fully.

The grace of God surrounds me, and I gratefully accept my blessings now. Day or night, whenever I feel down emotionally, I turn to God and receive the assurance of continual, eternal love and support.

Amazing grace strengthens and blesses me in even the most difficult times. Indeed, in each moment, I have new enthusiasm for life.

> "Of this gospel I have become a servant according
> to the gift of God's grace that was given me
> by the working of his power."
> —Ephesians 3:7

Rest

———◆———

*As I rest in the silence with God,
my body and my soul are restored.*

There are times when I feel so good physically, so
secure mentally that nothing can hold me back or shake
my confidence.

There may also be times when I have my doubts,
when I do not feel at my best or ready to make a
decision on an important matter. Yet even then I do not
worry, for I know that God will guide me moment by
moment in making decisions.

So I give myself a rest—in the silence with God.
Resting in God's presence clears my mind and relaxes
my body so that the flow of divine ideas and healing is
unimpaired. I am open to God's message of life and
wisdom. In the silence with God, my body and soul are
restored.

> "Stand at the crossroads, and look,
> and ask for the ancient paths,
> where the good way lies; and walk in it,
> and find rest for your souls."
> —Jeremiah 6:16

New Adventure

——◆——

*Every day is a new venture
in an adventure called life!*

Surely the heart of every great explorer was filled with anticipation, an excitement fed by both the challenge and fulfillment of a journey into the unknown.

My life itself is an adventure into the unknown, for I never know what may lie ahead. I, too, am an explorer who is given the promise of opportunity and adventure as God leads me in new ventures each day. God is my guide, and I know that whatever happens, God will give me the strength and the wisdom to be an active participant in life.

I seize the day and make the most of the life and intelligence that God has given me. I feel and express a zest for life that is rising from within me.

I am ready, willing, and eager to explore the marvelous blessings that God has in store for me throughout this amazing adventure called life!

"Do not lag in zeal, be ardent in spirit,
serve the Lord."
—Romans 12:11

Inner Peace

— ♦ —

Spiritually, physically, and emotionally,
I reflect the peace of God that is within me.

The peace that calms my soul, soothes my thoughts, and relaxes my body comes from one source, and that source is God. The good news is that the spirit of God is within me always; therefore, the peace of God is within me at all times.

I draw on this sacred reserve of peace in quiet communion with God throughout my daily routine. As I take these "peace breaks," I am renewed in spirit, mind, and body.

The peace I have within me is lived out through me as an ongoing communication of peace and harmony with others. As I interact with others throughout my day, I express the love of God in what I say and how I act.

The peace I feel in my heart is reflected on my face. My body glows with vitality, which is an outer reflection of the peace within my soul.

"I stand in the presence of God."
—Luke 1:19

God's Presence

———— ◆ ————

*I am safe and secure
in God's loving presence.*

I may tend to take for granted some of the things that make me feel secure—being in a home that is my haven of peace, being near family and friends, or having a telephone that connects me with people near and far.

Yet how secure do I feel when I am away from familiar people, places, and things? I know that there is no person or circumstance that can ever bring me more reassurance than the understanding that God is with me. God is a very real presence in my life, and I know that God will never fail me.

God is with me wherever I may go and in whatever I may be going through, helping me to make it through healthy and whole. I am forever in the care of my Creator.

> "He will command his angels concerning you
> to guard you in all your ways."
> —Psalms 91:11

Meditation

—◆—

"Seek the Lord and his strength,
seek his presence continually!"
—Psalms 105:4

In the silence of prayer and meditation, I take a
cool, calming breath and clear my mind of any
emotional clutter.

I turn away from any outer intrusions and
focus on the peace of God within. I take another
deep, calming breath, and then slowly release it. I
feel my body entering a relaxed state.

Continuing my rhythmic breathing, I touch my
hand to my heart. With my eyes closed and my
mind focused, I feel the beat of my heart as it
works with quiet strength.

My body is a wonderful work of God's
creativity. God has given me a priceless gift—the
gift of life.

I sit in silence, feeling the warm glow of life
throughout my entire being. As my time of prayer
comes to an end, I take another deep, cleansing
breath and whisper a prayer of thanks.

Prayer

*"I trust in you, O Lord;
I say, 'You are my God.'"*
—Psalms 31:14

God, my faith is in You, and I trust You to give me
whatever I need to live each moment fully and
without fear.

You have blessed me, God, with a strong body
and an intelligent mind. My body is a temple for
Your sacred spirit within, and I am grateful for the
ability to move from place to place with ease and
efficiency.

You also give me understanding, God; through
Your spirit within me I have a vital connection with
divine wisdom. I am shown how to care for my
body in ways that promote health and give
expression to Your radiant life within me.

As I think about the magnificent design of my
body, God, my faith is renewed and my trust in
my body's ability to heal itself is strengthened.
How could I ever doubt that You are with me?

Listen, Beloved

—◆—

Beloved,

You were created for life and health. Now claim your health and live your life fully.

Within this body that gives you shape and form, trillions of cells are being renewed. When you speak of life and healing, those cells respond with renewed life.

A virtual song of life is being played by you as your heart beats in a perfect rhythm that pulsates throughout your body.

There is a river of life flowing through you as a circulation of nourishment reaches every cell, muscle, and organ.

Keep this message of life and healing stored in your memory and listen to it often. I am the creator of all life—life I have given you and through which I am renewing you in every moment.

"My child, be attentive to my words. . . .
Keep them within your heart."
—Proverbs 4:20–21

Blessed Assurance

—◆—

*I am guided on my life's journey
by the light of God.*

Although it seems as if the light of the sun goes out as it disappears beyond the horizon each night, it is actually shining brightly on another part of the world. The power of the sun's light is never diminished.

The guiding light of God shines continuously as well. If I seem to be lost and in the dark concerning a health or emotional dilemma, it is not that the light of God has gone away. Rather, it is that I need to turn toward the divine light that is always shining brightly for me, revealing my way.

God assures me that I can and will find a guiding light for every day of my journey. All I need to do is turn to it in faith. Then I see clearly the path I am meant to take. As I rely on divine power and wisdom, I am guided out of the dark and into the light of a new day.

**"Come, let us walk
in the light of the Lord!"
—Isaiah 2:5**

Free

——◆——

*God gently guides me to freedom
and new opportunities.*

Every door serves a dual purpose—as an exit from one place and as an entrance to another.

If I need healing from a dependency or some other negative habit, I remember that God will guide me to freedom. As I move away from bad habits, I am also moving toward a future of new opportunities.

God does not force me to change. Rather, I am gently guided to an open door of possibilities. Because I trust God, I will follow through with a change.

As I step out of the past and into a new beginning, I leave behind those things that may limit me physically and mentally. I enter into a new dawn as a free being! I have listened to God and opened the door to a new life and a new me!

**"Into your hand I commit my spirit;
you have redeemed me, O Lord, faithful God."
—Psalms 31:5**

Comfort

———◆———

In God's loving presence,
I am comforted and renewed.

In the silence of prayer, I turn to the One who gives me strength and soothes my troubled heart.

In God's loving presence, I am at peace. I have connected on a heart-and-soul level with a peace that surpasses all human understanding—a peace that comforts me and takes my mind off what is making me sad or anxious. Then my attention is focused on the love that is with me always.

In God's loving presence, my strength is renewed. I can literally feel divine life as it works its way through the muscles and organs of my body and gives me the courage and strength to go on. I know that I can go on—to a future that is filled with life and hope.

> "Everlasting joy shall be upon their heads;
> they shall obtain joy and gladness,
> and sorrow and sighing shall flee away.
> I, am he who comforts you."
> —Isaiah 51:11–12

TODAY'S MESSAGE:
Seeing Clearly

—◆—

*The reassurance, love, and guidance of God
bring clarity to my life.*

Like an image being developed on photographic paper,
some solutions in life take time to unfold with clarity.

During times of challenge, I move forward in faith,
and confusion gives way to understanding. What may
have seemed like a problem yesterday, I now recognize
is an opportunity for me to bring my full attention to
God.

Out of what I perceived to be a most difficult time, I
made tremendous leaps in spiritual growth. This was
possible because I never have to go through anything
without the reassurance, love, and guidance of God.

Nothing can break me down when I allow the spirit
of God to build me up. Knowing in every moment that
the life of God strengthens me, the wisdom of God
guides me, and the love of God inspires me, I see my
life clearly.

> "For now we see in a mirror, dimly,
> but then we will see face to face."
> —1 Corinthians 13:12

DAILY WORD FOR HEALING

Forgive

———◆———

*Through forgiveness, I release the past
and begin anew.*

Just as the new year is a time for leaving the past behind
and beginning again, so forgiveness is a way of
releasing emotional pain so that I can be healed and
move on.

So I forgive. With all my heart and soul, I bless the
person or situation that has caused me pain and then
gently release it. I realize that it is not my place to judge
or condemn anyone. But my forgiveness has the power
to set me and the other person free to move forward
and be healthier in our individual lives.

Wherever my life may lead me, it is God's love
working through me that helps me to forgive. And
through forgiveness, I open my mind and heart to the
healing power of God—a power that moves in
miraculous ways to bless me.

"Do not judge, and you will not be judged;
do not condemn, and you will not be condemned.
Forgive, and you will be forgiven."
—Luke 6:37

Mind and Body

— ◆ —

*My mind and body work together
in a harmony of life.*

If I am worried or feeling stressed, my thinking is certainly affected negatively, and my body may suffer as well.

My mind and body, however, can work together in a harmonious activity that promotes healing. The nerves and cells of my body respond to the energy of positive thoughts, and these thoughts create beneficial responses.

So I remember that God is always with me and that divine order is constantly being established in my life. Knowing this, why would I worry?

As the activity of my mind slows, thoughts of peace and divine assurance rush in. My body is relieved of tension. My life-affirming thoughts help me to heal. Now, mind and body are working together in harmony and expressing divine life.

"The spirit of God has made me,
and the breath of the Almighty gives me life."
—Job 33:4

Sacred Identity

——◆——

I am blessed with a spiritual identity.

Jesus helped people look past their own doubts about themselves and their worthiness to the sacredness of their souls. He shared this vision of holiness and wholeness with all people.

Perhaps more than ever, my self-esteem may be lacking because I am being inundated with images and ideas of how I should look or sound or feel in order to fit into society.

I know how to make such doubt take wing and leave my thoughts: I stop doubting by recognizing my own sacredness. This precious identity cannot be earned or bought or learned. It is a gift from God.

I am a sacred being, worthy of every blessing of life and healing that God has in store for me! And this sacred identity is the true identity of each person. Although we may look and speak differently, we are all spiritual beings.

> "So God created humankind in his image,
> in the image of God he created them."
> —Genesis 1:27

Enfolded in God's Presence

—◆—

*God's presence fills me and enfolds me
with life and love.*

I am God's creation of life! In all things, in all ways, and at all times, I know that God is with me.

God was with me during all the past events of my life. Looking back now, I clearly understand that I have been divinely protected and guided all along the way. Having gone through both challenges and achievements, I have grown stronger and wiser.

I have faith that God is with me right now. I do not need physical evidence to prove that God's presence fills me and enfolds me with life and love. Faith assures me that God is with me always.

The spirit of God lives within me and renews me with life. I greet each day with faith because I know I am enfolded in God's presence.

"There is one body and one Spirit . . .
one God and Father of all, who is above all
and through all and in all."
—Ephesians 4:4,6

Meditation

—◆—

*"But as for me, my prayer is to you, O Lord.
At an acceptable time, O God,
in the abundance of your steadfast love,
answer me."*
—*Psalms 69:13*

In the sacred activity of prayer, I leave behind any concerns about symptoms of illness so that I will be fully in the presence of God.

In God's loving presence, I understand more and more that God is the answer to my prayers for myself and my loved ones.

My faith is in God, and I let faith guide me in being open to all the things that are best for me and for them.

I may have heard or read about some way of improving our well-being, but God speaks to me about what blesses us most. I listen for a gentle whisper as I sit in the silence.

My faith assures me that God listens to and answers my every prayer. However my inspiration comes, I follow through on it with a dedicated heart and soul.

Prayer

"The Lord of hosts is with us."
—Psalms 46:11

God, I understand that sometimes my prayers may not be answered in the way that I would have chosen, but I know that all things happen for a reason.

The answer to a healing prayer for myself or my loved ones can come in many forms, and I recognize that Your wisdom is always at work in our lives. If someone I love is dealing with a serious threat to his or her health, I keep in mind that You know what is best.

Losing loved ones is so painful, but I gain peace of mind knowing that my loved ones are never lost to me or You. They are eternally enfolded in Your loving care where there is no pain or suffering—only love and peace.

God, Your wisdom governs my life and the lives of my loved ones, and I trust in You.

Listen, Beloved

—◆—

Beloved,

Some of your greatest moments were when you were going through your greatest challenges. You did not let anyone or anything defeat you. When symptoms or a diagnosis proclaimed your health was deteriorating, you believed in your health and claimed a healing. And you were healed.

There is light in the darkness—My light shining from you and those around you. If ever you feel lost or lonely, imagine yourself opening the door of your soul. Feel the warmth of My love as light shining upon you.

Challenges never are as challenging as they appear. Learn to look for and discover the good that comes from every situation. Good is there, for I am there.

My delight, beloved, is giving you unlimited blessings. Within every dark moment, My light is shining in you and in those for whom you pray.

"The light shines in the darkness,
and the darkness did not overcome it."
—John 1:5

Making Decisions

—◆—

*My choices are inspired by God
in the quiet of prayer.*

Each day I make hundreds of choices—prioritizing activities and responsibilities into a full schedule for the day.

Some days I give more thought to routine things—what I will wear and eat—but not all of my choices are routine. Some are of greater significance because they concern my own well-being and the well-being of my family, my job, or my finances. So whenever a choice seems difficult, I take it to God in prayer.

In the quiet of my soul, God waits for me. As I enter the sanctuary of my soul—a sacred place of prayer—I leave behind all concern and doubt. In silence, God speaks to me in a language of the soul.

I have turned to God within me for understanding, and now I have the confidence to make decisions that enhance my life and the lives of my loved ones.

> "The human mind plans the way,
> but the Lord directs the steps."
> —Proverbs 16:9

Spirit-Filled Life

—◆—

*I am blessed with the riches
of a spirit-filled life.*

When I take a moment to appreciate the blessings I
have received, I understand that I have been blessed in
ways I never would have dreamed were possible for
me. God has given me an abundance of blessings.

Both friends and family have richly blessed me.
Although relationships are not always easy, I am drawn
to people who help bring out the best in me and in
whom I help bring out the best. We care about and for
one another.

My body blesses me—it is a marvelous creation of
God. I do not need to remind my heart, lungs, or other
organs to function. Without my having to ask, God
provides air for me to breathe.

Yes, it is true—my prosperity is so much more than
material things or financial matters. My prosperity
knows no bounds, for God continues to bless me
every day.

**"In all that they do, they prosper."
—Psalms 1:3**

Treasures of the Heart

———◆———

The treasures within my heart are everlasting joy
living out through me.

The treasures that I have stored in my heart bring joy to
me now. Jesus understood this and shared the light of
divine understanding with the people who gathered
around Him, saying, "Where your treasure is, there your
heart will be also" (Matthew 6:21).

What do I treasure and store in my heart? I treasure
the priceless blessings that God gives to me freely and
lovingly: Life-affirming thoughts are treasures of the
heart, and my awareness of God and the power of God
to heal me is a treasure worth more than any amount of
money could buy or any great achievement could earn
me. Tender times with family and friends are treasures I
can relive over and over again in thought.

Oh, what joy my treasures are to me! They are
everlasting joy living out through me as experiences of
my divine reality.

> **"For where your treasure is,**
> **there your heart will be also."**
> **—Matthew 6:21**

Divine Love

———◆———

*Divine love is constantly nourishing
and healing me.*

Like a free-flowing river, the love of God is constantly
moving in and through all life. Divine love is a gentle
yet powerful stream—a healing force that nourishes me,
refreshes my relationships, and renews my body.

Whenever I feel stuck and not able to move forward
with my life, I am lifted and carried along by this stream
of love. Because I trust God, I release every concern,
every burden, and rest in the love of God. I experience
how truly wonderful it feels to be held securely in the
tender embrace of God's love.

I am calm, and my body fairly shouts with the joy of
being stress-free. Every cell is stimulated, and I am
renewed. How completely the love of God heals and
blesses me!

> "But I am like a green olive tree
> in the house of God.
> I trust in the steadfast love of God
> forever and ever."
> —Psalms 52:8

Stand Firm

—◆—

I stand firm in my faith in God and in my divine heritage of eternal life and freedom.

There is nothing in the world powerful enough to take away my divine heritage—the eternal life and freedom that God has given me. Divine life renews me moment by moment, and divine freedom lets me know in my heart what is the right thing for me to do.

So I stand firm in my faith in God's plan for me. I let go of doubt and fear and remain true to my belief that with God, anything is possible for me—from minor changes in my routine to miraculous healings.

As I stand with God, I am proclaiming life and my freedom to live life. God's love is a powerful presence that I hold on to in even the most stressful situations.

With God, I am free! I embrace that freedom now and throughout all eternity!

> "Do not be afraid, stand firm, and see
> the deliverance that the Lord
> will accomplish for you today."
> —Exodus 14:13

Healing Words

———◆———

*The words I speak are words
of life and healing.*

Every positive, life-affirming word has the power to
both soothe and heal. So each day—wherever I am—
I do my part to make a positive difference in my family,
workplace, and community by helping to create an
atmosphere of love through words of healing.

As I speak words of compassion and understanding,
I am opening the door to a healing of relationships.
Kind words promote peace and generate love in all
circumstances.

My own experience of generating life-affirming
thoughts has been so important to me in maintaining
my own health that I just naturally want to share my
blessings with others. By speaking faith-filled words of
life and health to and about my friends and loved ones,
I am supporting them in their healing and recovery.

"The tongue of the wise brings healing."
—Proverbs 12:18

Strength of Spirit

— ◆ —

*I am strong in the life, love,
and spirit of God.*

Do I love and appreciate myself as a unique creation of the God of all creation? Of course I do! What I love about myself is the magnificent spiritual being that is living through my physical body.

I also appreciate my humanness, which enables me to show love through words and hugs, to give the tender touch of caring to others.

This is the day I let my spiritual nature come forward in all its power and glory. Now I can and do eliminate any habit or tendency that might have been getting in the way of my experiencing a wholeness of spirit, mind, and body. I know that in giving up negative thoughts, I am giving more of myself and my attention to God.

I am strong in the life, love, and spirit of God.

> "But those who wait for the Lord
> shall renew their strength, they shall mount up
> with wings like eagles."
> —Isaiah 40:31

Golden Moments

—◆—

*I cherish the memories
of the golden moments of my life.*

The times I cherish most are ones that bring me special joy. These are golden moments in which God reveals the purpose of life and how I can enhance my life.

Yet I know every moment in life has purpose. Behind both chance encounters and well-planned events, there is an opportunity for me to discover a divine plan that is charged with goodness for me and for my path in life.

So I look at each experience as I imagine God would see it—filled with opportunities for me to learn and grow. From this perspective, I am able to welcome seemingly routine and unusual experiences, recognizing the blessings they hold for me.

Each moment of every day is a golden moment from God—a time to live life fully and be aware of all the beauty and wonder of life.

"Out of the north comes golden splendor;
around God is awesome majesty."
—Job 37:22

GIVING BACK TO LIFE
BY JULIE HANNA

M y heart ached as I looked into one of the most beautiful faces I had ever seen. Sasha, a male snow leopard, was brought to the zoo where I worked when he was about 3 weeks old, but something was terribly wrong with him. His chest was caved in, pushing his heart against his lungs. Sasha had such diffi- culty breathing that the veterinarian had decided to eu- thanize him.

Looking at Sasha, I felt an overwhelming desire to help him. I didn't want to give up on him, because I knew the miracle that had happened when people didn't give up on me. I had made it, and Sasha could too.

When I was 2 years old, I was diagnosed with leukemia. At that time, not many children survived this disease. My parents heard of an experimental treatment that was being done at St. Jude's Hospital in Memphis, so they took me there. Because this was a cancer research center, the treatment the other children and I received was determined by a lottery system: Whichever treatment was on the card drawn for a child was the treatment he or she received.

My draw was the most aggressive treatment, which consisted of spinal injections of methotrexate, massive dosages of radiation to the brain, and chemotherapy drugs.

In isolation for 3 months, I was able to see my family and they could see me through a glass wall, but we couldn't touch. My mother never left the hospital, and my dad brought my two sisters to see me often.

There were 12 patients on my floor, and I was one of only two who survived. Because of the massive dosages of radiation received as children, a few people developed brain tumors later in life. In June of 1995, I got sick and doctors discovered that I had a brain tumor—the size of an orange—which had pushed the front half of my brain to the back hemisphere.

The night before I had surgery, my parents and friends gathered around me as my long hair was cut to a short, pixie style. The love they surrounded me with helped turn the loss of my hair into a fun time. One of the most calming moments came when we joined hands and our minister led us in a prayer of surrender: We turned everything over to God. The following day, my head was shaved and I underwent surgery that lasted 9 hours.

I knew that four other patients who had been treated at the children's hospital for leukemia had developed brain tumors—and all were malignant. After my surgery, however, I received good news. My oncologist said: "Julie, your Heavenly Father is looking after you. The tumor was benign."

I have been extremely blessed by the Lord, having survived two life-threatening diseases. Maybe my greatest blessing has been having such a wonderful family to help me through it all. My mom and dad as well as my two sisters and their husbands were always there for me. And I especially needed them when I felt depressed. I appreciated all the cards I received and all the prayers my family, friends, and other people offered for me.

I have lived a long life in a short time. And I realize it's not the material things around me that are important; it's the love and support I have been given.

I have asked myself why I was saved twice, but I don't have the answer. After my brain surgery, although I was not always totally aware, I remember hearing that other children and adults in the neurosurgery ward had not made it. I wanted somehow to be able to give part of my life to them, but I didn't know how.

When Sasha came into my life, I had an opportunity to give love and support back to life through one of God's endangered creatures.

This was about a year after I had brain surgery. I was going to summer school, doing homework, working at the zoo, and taking care of Sasha, which was a 24-hour job in itself. I was up every few hours during the night feeding him, giving him antibiotics, and massaging his stomach to help move his food through. Sasha responded beautifully: Within 6 months his chest filled out, and he has grown into a magnificent adult snow leopard.

Taking care of Sasha brought me so much joy. In fact, taking care of all baby animals fills my life with joy. Like all of us, they respond to the love and care they are given. They don't care what we look like; they just accept us for who we are, and they accept all the love we are willing to give them. They know, as well as we do, that love is the most important gift we can give one another.

Spirit of Giving

———◆———

Giving from the spirit of God within me,
I am more.

What more do I want from life? Is it more love, money, or recognition?

Intuitively, I know that having more things or greater financial security will never satisfy the yearning of my soul or fill my heart and mind with unshakable peace. I realize that what I really desire is to *give* more to life. As I give from the abundance of God in me and in my world, I become more. I am capable of doing more and being more.

The universe is made of the very particles of life that make up me; I am a creation of God in a universe of God's creation. So it's only natural that I have a deep desire to be a blessing.

I can be a blessing by letting God move through me in what I think, say, and do. Then I give the very best to my family, my friends, and my world.

Filled to overflowing with the rejuvenating presence of God, my awareness of the divine has no limits.

"From this day on I will bless you."
—Haggai 2:19

Vital to My Health

—◆—

I am whole and healthy in mind and body.

Knowing that the mind-body connection is vital to my health, I think positive thoughts and speak life-affirming words that bless my body.

I bless my heart. I pray and I visualize my heart as the strong and healthy organ God created it to be. With each beat of my heart, my entire body is nourished.

I bless my lungs. As I relax and take in air, my lungs expand effortlessly with the breath of life. I am invigorated with life. And as I breathe out, I release all worries and negative thoughts.

I bless my eyes and my ears. They are the precious instruments with which I view my world and am in communication with it. I give thanks to God for the wondrous work that my eyes and ears do.

I bless my entire body. I feel God-life responding to my positive prayers and thoughts as both my body and confidence are strengthened. I am whole and healthy in mind and body.

"The words that I say to you I do not speak on my own; but the Father who dwells in me does his works."
—John 14:10

Celebrate Life!

— ◆ —

*Renewed and healed,
I celebrate life!*

In the parable of the prodigal son, the youngest son left his family. Over time, this young man made so many errors in judgment that he was left with nothing (Luke 15:11–32).

Broke and ashamed, he started the journey home; however, the moment the father saw his son, he ran out to greet him. In a grand celebration, the father helped his son put the past behind him, heal his emotional wounds, and begin again.

I, too, can release the past and the mistakes I have made. And I, too, have reason to celebrate, for every day is a chance to heal and to begin anew. Today I celebrate the first day of a new life for me. God has given me the kingdom—a kingdom that includes an abundance of life, love, and peace. In a celebration of life, I accept the blessings of life with a grateful heart.

> "'Let us eat and celebrate; for this son of mine
> was dead and is alive again; he was lost and is found!'
> And they began to celebrate."
> —Luke 15:23–24

Flexible

—◆—

*Because I am flexible, I am tender and strong,
resilient and grounded.*

There is great strength in being flexible. For instance, it's amazing to watch how a tender sapling survives a hard wind by moving with the wind instead of resisting it.

When the winds of challenge and change rush at me, I can remain flexible by using the wisdom God has given me. I do not waste my energy and time trying to control circumstances or people. Rather, I let God guide my actions and know that God will give me the wisdom and understanding that will enable me to overcome challenges.

Yes, I am flexible. And because I am, I know that I can also be tender and strong, resilient and grounded. Praise God!

"The wind blows where it chooses, and you hear
the sound of it, but you do not know where it comes
from or where it goes. So it is with everyone who
is born of the Spirit."
—John 3:8

I Am Willing

—◆—

I am a willing participant in life.

How honored I am to be an original God-creation and a member of God's family!

God has entrusted me with this life that I am living, and because I am so blessed, I am willing to do my best in living it.

I am willing to express love for all humankind. I can because God has given my heart an unlimited capacity for giving and receiving love.

I am willing to express peace at all times. My actions and words are inspired by divine love. Therefore, I am compassionate and kind, thoughtful and considerate.

I am willing to lend a helping hand whenever someone needs support during a crisis or concerning everyday matters. The desire to help make someone's day a bit easier flows from my willing heart, and I remain willing to do my best with the life God has given me.

> "I will praise the Lord as long as I live;
> I will sing praises to my God all my life long."
> —Psalms 146:2

The Peace of God

———◆———

*God's peace, which surpasses all understanding,
fills my heart and mind.*

Like the gentle breeze of summer, the peace of God
sweeps over my soul. I invite this peace—a peace that
surpasses all human understanding—into my heart
and mind.

Gently—yet, oh, so powerfully—peace moves
throughout my body, relaxing me. Because I am
relaxed, there is a free flow through my circulatory
system that nourishes me.

Like a soothing balm, God's peace eases the pain.
God whispers a message of love and healing that
penetrates into the very cells of my body. And my
body's answer to the call of God-life within is healing.

Filled with the peace of God, I am grateful for my
healing.

"Do not worry about anything, but in everything
by prayer and supplication with thanksgiving let
your requests be made known to God. And the peace
of God, which surpasses all understanding,
will guard your hearts and your minds."
—Philippians 4:6–7

TODAY'S MESSAGE:
Faith Builder

———◆———

*My life is an unfolding work
of faith.*

Perhaps, more than anything else, I need something to bolster my faith today. So I remember Jesus' words to His disciples: "Have faith in God" (Mark 11:22).

This powerful reminder speaks to me now in this very moment, encouraging me in a faith that uplifts my thoughts. I move from thinking about the size and complexity of a challenge to the power and presence of God in the midst of me and in everything that concerns me.

Having faith in God does not change God, but it does change me. My view of all things takes on the added glow of spiritual understanding. My faith in God brings clarity to the most confusing situations.

I am making my life a work of faith and discovering the blessings that are everywhere present in my world.

> "Jesus answered them,
> 'Have faith in God.'"
> —Mark 11:22

Delight

——◆——

*I am delighted with life and all the unique
and diverse expressions of life.*

Laughing has been called inner jogging. I feel that is what happens when I laugh. My whole body reacts to laughter and delight with a wonderful, freeing response. It's as if the trillions of cells throughout my body are experiencing a workout.

How good it is to laugh and to share laughter with others. I thank God for the ability to laugh and for giving me a way to show my delight with all the diverse expressions of life.

Sometimes laughter is a personal response to something I am feeling or observing. At other times, laughter is a union of joy I share with others. Amazingly, there need be no other reason for laughter than the pure joy of expressing gladness.

> "Make a joyful noise to the Lord, all the earth.
> Worship the Lord with gladness;
> come into his presence with singing."
> —Psalms 100:1–2

Meditation

—◆—

"Glorify God in your body."
—1 Corinthians 6:20

In my meditation time today, I envision myself entering a place—a chapel, a garden, a candlelit room—in which the atmosphere of art, nature, or aromas enhances my awareness of God.

In prayer, I enter a sacred place where I am absolutely aware that God and I are one. I feel this whole and holy union with my Creator in every fiber of my being.

I am blessed by my awareness of God. God's spirit is within me, and I now immerse myself in the presence of God that surrounds me. From the top of my head to the soles of my feet, I am fully enveloped by the presence of God.

I visualize the celebration of life that is taking place within my soul and within my body. I feel renewed and serene. I know I could move effortlessly, but still I do not want to move. I want to linger for a while in this sacred awareness and bless my whole body with a time of healing and renewal.

DAILY WORD FOR HEALING

Prayer

— ◆ —

*"In him was life, and the life
was the light of all people."*
—John 1:4

Sweet Spirit of life, Your strength enlivens me.
With every beat of my heart, Your healing,
renewing life flows to the tissues and organs that
support me, allowing me to perform physical tasks
smoothly and easily. Thank You, sweet Spirit, for a
miraculously created body and for a life-support
system that sustains me!

Your life within, sweet Spirit, provides me with
the energy to make it through any challenge. You
are the source of all life, and my vital connection
with You can never be broken—even when a
health challenge seems to indicate otherwise. If
such a situation arises, I take my mind off the
challenge and focus instead on Your life within me.
Immediately I feel a shift—from the discomfort of
thinking about "dis-ease" and chaos to the
experience of peace of mind. I am restored!

Listen, Beloved

—◆—

Beloved,

You and I are one. My spirit within you is a vital connection that surpasses all that is known and observed in the physical realm.

You have the ability to think clearly and respond without hesitation. If you are worried that you will not remember what is important to you—such as the names of the people you interact with, the answers to a test, or where you left your keys—simply let go and let Me give you the answers you seek.

Through a divine connection, you have access to all the wisdom, inspiration, and guidance you need to make wise decisions—decisions that will lead you in a healthy, fulfilling life.

Trust in Me, beloved, and rely on My wisdom to guide you through every moment of the day.

"God gave Solomon very great wisdom,
discernment, and breadth of understanding
as vast as the sand on the seashore."
—1 Kings 4:29

Knowing God

—— ◆ ——

I know more of God when I love as God loves—
unconditionally.

My greatest blessing is knowing God. My awareness of
God and my understanding of the divine presence
within me have opened the way for inspiration and
healing.

Yet what can I do that would help me to know God
more—to increase my awareness of God? I can and do
continue to spend time every day in prayer—opening
my mind and heart and listening as God speaks to me.
Another sure way to know more of God is to love as
God does—unconditionally.

So I let God love through me. The more loving I am
to others, the more I am letting God into my heart and
learning what God's nature is. Loving thought by loving
thought, my awareness of God grows—and I receive
more of the inspiration, healing, and peace I desire.

> "Love is from God; everyone who loves
> is born of God and knows God."
> —1 John 4:7

Spiritual Understanding

—◆—

*The spirit of God within me is my freedom
to live life fully!*

I plan to live this day fully, so I avoid letting my thoughts and memories take me back to living in the past. I have come through events and circumstances a stronger and wiser person, and I can be free of feelings of regret or resentment about mistakes or mishaps that I have experienced.

The spirit of God within me gives me the understanding to look at my life with spiritual discernment. Such a vision allows me to decide what to leave behind and what to bring with me to each new day. I release what is no longer in my best interest and hold on to what helps me step into the future with confidence and enhanced health.

The past is the past, and today is now. Today and every day, I am free with the freedom of Spirit. I live freely and fully the life that God has given me to live.

> **"The law of the Spirit of life
> in Christ Jesus has set you free."
> —Romans 8:2**

Renewed

— ◆ —

*My Creator is continually
renewing me with life.*

I may think of springtime as a natural, yearly wake-up call to the renewal of life.

Because of the beauty, color, textures, and fragrances in its panorama, I can never take any spring for granted. I know that this rebirth in nature is a divine design for all life, which includes me.

Just as surely as spring returns to the earth with a resurgence of life, so does a season of spring and renewal come to me. By knowing that I am included in the renewal of life, I accept the new seasons of life for myself and the experiences they offer me.

In fact, every season of life is a time of renewal and strengthening for me, because God created me and is continually renewing me with life.

"Oh Lord my God, you are very great. . . .
When you send forth your spirit, they are created;
and you renew the face of the ground."
—Psalms 104:1, 30

Wonder of God

———◆———

*I behold the wonder
of God's presence within me.*

When I look at the world around me, I can't help but be impressed by such a magnificent display of life and creativity. I am filled with awe at the wonder of all that God has created.

With spiritual understanding, I perceive the wonder that is within—the miracle of my own soul. I feel such a great exhilaration in knowing that the spirit of God is within me and that I am giving expression to the sacredness of life.

Each reminder of God's presence in me and in the world inspires me. The assurance of God's love rises up from within in quiet moments of prayer. The brilliant hues of a sunrise remind me to let the light of God within shine out into the world.

> "Whatever God does endures forever; nothing can be added to it, nor anything taken from it; God has done this, so that all should stand in awe before him."
> —Ecclesiastes 3:14

Still Me

——◆——

*I am a creation of God, and I am capable
of great achievements every day.*

Physical changes happen that may alter my appearance.
No matter how much I change on the outside, though,
I am still "me" on the inside. My soul is flourishing
because the spirit of God resides there.

Neither situations nor people around me control who
I am. I am certain of the real me because God is
sustaining me.

If a situation should present itself that seems
insurmountable, I remain confident. I am still me—still
capable of learning more of what I can achieve. And
God is with me to see me through.

God is expressing life through me. I thank God for
the security of knowing that no matter what I go
through, I will always be God's creation. This is my true
identity—the real me.

"For we are what he has made us, created
in Christ Jesus for good works, which God prepared
beforehand to be our way of life."
—Ephesians 2:10

Healthy Attitude

—◆—

God is healing me!

When I am praying about a health challenge, I naturally want to feel and see the improvement immediately. The sooner, the better!

Yet I do not lose hope; I know that my healing can come in an instant or over the course of time. I have peace of mind because I know that my healing is taking place through the spirit of God within me.

I facilitate my own healing by thinking positive thoughts, by taking time for both rest and exercise, and by eating healthy, nutritious food.

Healing life is flowing through me, renewing every cell of my body and energizing me. I thank God for the healing that is taking place. My positive thoughts and actions are a continuation of my attitude of gratefulness.

God is healing me. My belief in God's healing power soothes me and opens me to complete healing.

> **"I will call to mind the deeds of the Lord;**
> **I will remember your wonders of old."**
> **—Psalms 77:11**

Divine Embrace

———◆———

*I am enfolded in a divine embrace
that comforts and supports me.*

There are times when I just want to be alone. It is not that I don't appreciate others or the help they would give me—I do—but I also know in my heart that the only one who can find the right answer for me is me.

Then there are those times when only a hug will do. I feel so reassured in knowing that even when I am alone, I am held within God's loving embrace. No matter where I am, God is with me to love and support me.

God's tender embrace comforts me through every challenge of life. In God's loving embrace there is nothing to fear—for I am resting in the presence of the One who provides the very shelter that keeps me safe all the days of my life.

> "The beloved of the Lord rests in safety—
> the High God surrounds him all day long—
> the beloved rests between His shoulders."
> —Deuteronomy 33:12

Healing Touch

—◆—

*I bless others with the healing touch
of kindness.*

Some pain encountered in the human experience is best relieved by the healing touch of kindness.

For instance, if someone I know is lonely or withdrawn, a reassuring word from me can be a soothing balm. Just knowing that someone cares may be the perfect remedy for the person who is feeling rejected.

I care enough about others to show them I care. My words of encouragement and support are sweet music to those needing to hear that they are loved and appreciated.

By extending my hand in friendship and by encouraging others, I am establishing a lifeline of communication and companionship. By giving my time and attention to others and applying the healing touch of kindness, I can make a positive difference in their lives.

"Be kind to one another, tenderhearted, forgiving one another, as God in Christ has forgiven you."
—Ephesians 4:32

Meditation

—◆—

"I will make a covenant of peace with them; it shall be an everlasting covenant with them, and I will bless them and multiply them, and will set my sanctuary among them forevermore."
—*Ezekiel 37:26*

Even during the busiest of times, there is a quiet place that I can retreat to—a place where concerns are left behind and I am totally aware of being in the presence of God.

This quiet place is nearer than the air I breathe, for it lies within the depths of my soul. Turning within, I feel the peace of God surrounding me.

Enfolded in peace, I experience how it feels to have every nerve soothed and my mind swept clean of confusion. Once again I am focused on my source of life and living—the presence of God.

No person or circumstance can disrupt the peace I feel in the quiet with God. I return from this sanctuary of peace renewed, refreshed, and revitalized in mind, body, and spirit.

Prayer

—◆—

"He leads me in right paths."
—Psalms 23:3

God, giving my complete awareness to You in prayer, I am at peace.

In Your presence, I am filled to overflowing with Your love and inspired to be a shining example of how a person lives, thinks, and acts in oneness with You.

You are my wisdom and my life, and I am in awe of the love and care with which You have blessed me. I feel Your spirit moving through me as a healing energy that gently awakens me to the power and potential that are within me.

I know that worry will never solve the questions of my heart, so I release all concern to You. Health, prosperity, relationships—whatever challenge I am facing, I know that peace flows from Your spirit within me.

Thank You, God.

Listen, Beloved

—◆—

Beloved,

Come to Me in any time of need, and I will soothe your soul.

My love for you is unconditional and without end. There is nothing you have ever done or said that has or could have lessened My love for you.

Let Me ease your mind of anxiety and pain. As you allow My love and peace into your mind and heart, you will experience a healing of emotions that brings you blessed relief.

Do not doubt yourself, beloved, or feel that you are not worthy of the very best life has to offer. You are one of My sacred creations, and you have an important contribution to make through your life and the way you live it.

Whenever you have a need, I have the answer, because I am the answer. I will give you the comfort and strength you need.

"I will turn their mourning into joy,
I will comfort them,
and give them gladness for sorrow."
—Jeremiah 31:13

DAILY WORD FOR HEALING

Surprise!
—◆—

*God is blessing me in both expected
and unexpected ways.*

I may have certain expectations about myself and my health for today and for the future. Yet even though I am as positive as I can be, I never let my own ideas and expectations limit the good that God has for me.

God is continually blessing me in expected and unexpected ways. Many times, it is in the unexpected blessings that I find the answers I have been seeking to a fuller life—spiritually, physically, and emotionally.

I am ready for each miracle, each unexpected blessing that happens. I welcome each experience—planned or unplanned—as an opportunity for God to bless me even more.

I am always being blessed, because I am always learning more about God. I see myself and my life with a new vision—one that looks for the good in each situation.

"Amazement seized all of them,
and they glorified God and were filled with awe."
—Luke 5:26

Endings and Beginnings

———◆———

*Thank You, God, for all the good
in this day and in every day.*

Holding fast to my faith, I know that every ending has a new beginning. Old ways of thinking and living must be released before new ideas for healthy living can take root in my life. In overcoming bad habits or dependencies, old associations must give way to new ones.

Revitalizing a relationship can happen as I let past grievances and resentments die away. Bringing greater love and understanding to my relationships leads to healthier communication, which could lead to a new beginning in a relationship that may have seemed at an end.

All this and more can take place as I place my faith in God. Then God gives back to me through a new beginning in which a healthier lifestyle is revealed.

> "Then Jesus, crying with a loud voice, said,
> 'Father, into your hands I commend my spirit.'"
> —Luke 23:46

Healthy Digestion

— ◆ —

*Being at peace as I eat, I aid in the digestion
of my food. I am nourished and satisfied.*

My digestive system is both complex and efficient—
moving food through my body and processing it so that
it is absorbed as nourishment.

Starting my day with prayer and a nutritious breakfast
infuses me with energy. I help with the digestion of the
food I eat by eating food that promotes health, by
chewing my food well, and by remaining calm while I
eat and after I eat.

The inner peace I experience as I eat goes a long way
in helping my body make good use of the nutrition it is
receiving. So I bless my food in prayer and do all that I
can to ensure that mealtimes with family and friends are
pleasant interludes in which our conversation adds
flavor to the food.

When I am eating alone, I select nutritious food with
colors and textures that brighten my plate and also
brighten my mealtime experience.

"You shall eat the fruit of the labor of your hands;
you shall be happy, and it shall go well with you."
—Psalms 128:2

Spirit of God

— ◆ —

The spirit of God is in all and through all
as healing, renewing life.

When I touch my face, my shoulders, my arms, or any other part of my body, I know that I am touching the visible, physical form of an invisible, spiritual being. The life-giving spirit of God flows continuously throughout my body, renewing and revitalizing me in response to the life-giving call of Spirit.

The spirit of God is in all and through all as healing, renewing life. So if I or a member of my family needs God's healing touch, I remember that the spirit of God is already working in and through us to revitalize every cell and organ of our bodies.

I am a spiritual being of God's creation. Day by day, I am coming to a greater understanding of who I am and the power of God's healing presence within me and others. Oh, how great it is to celebrate life and Spirit!

> "He has risen."
> —Mark 16:6 (RSV)

TODAY'S MESSAGE:
Relief

——◆——

*I forgive and experience relief
of heart and soul.*

I may not realize that I am carrying the burden of
resentment or anger within me, yet I know that
something is not right with me and with my life.

So if I am feeling down, I do something that lifts me
up: I forgive. I forgive myself for anything I have done
that did not bring glory to God. With that forgiveness, I
renew my dedication to living as a child of God and
experience relief of heart and soul.

I forgive others—whether or not they are still a part
of my life. They may not have been the loving people
I needed them to be when I was a child or as an adult,
but I forgive them. As I forgive, I release the hurt and
disappointments of the past, free myself to feel better,
and free them to do better. I am on my way to a
healthier me and healthier relationships with the ones
I love.

"If anyone has a complaint against another,
forgive each other; just as the Lord has forgiven you,
so you also must forgive."
—Colossians 3:13

God's Love

— ◆ —

*God's love is being poured out
to me constantly.*

The love of God is powerfully reflected in me; yet this
does not mean that I will never have to go through
times of challenge and growth.

I know from experience, however, that the very times
I am challenged most are the times when I am inspired
to let more of God live out through me. The more of
God I express, the more I recognize God's love moving
in and through my life.

As I open my heart to the love of God that is always
being poured out to me, I know that nothing can defeat
me. I become aware of the wonder of God in my life
every day. Then what may have seemed like a challenge
becomes an opportunity to let more of God be
expressed through me as love and ever-renewing life.

"I am convinced that neither death, nor life, nor angels,
nor rulers, nor things present, nor things to come . . .
will be able to separate us from the love of God."
—Romans 8:38–39

Fountain of Gladness

—◆—

God is my source of the joy
and gladness of my soul.

My happiness is so much more than an outpouring of laughter over a funny happening or the exhilaration of a good time with friends and family. Within my soul there is a quiet joy—a joy born of my faith in God.

I may not express inner joy so much with laughter as I do with an attitude of love and reverence for all people and all life.

My joy is a gladness of spirit, a sense of well-being, and strength in knowing my oneness with God. My heartfelt connection with God never fades, not even during situations that challenge me. The presence of God fills me with hope that blesses me in every moment of life.

My heart has been created with an unlimited capacity to express love. At the very center of my soul, the joy of Spirit dwells. God is my source of joy, a fountain of gladness that never runs dry.

"God, our God, has blessed us."
—Psalms 67:6

Affirming Life

———— ◆ ————

I am God's creation of life and health!

Speaking affirmations of life and healing aloud and silently reading them are important ways for me to help myself to remain healthy and also to heal.

For instance, when I say, "I am God's creation of life and health!" I am affirming the power of God's life within me. I am bringing my thoughts in line with the health and healing I desire to experience.

Using affirmations of life, I am not in denial about facts or circumstances; I am affirming the healing, renewing presence of God in me. What greater truth could I proclaim!

With each affirmation of life, I am proclaiming the presence and power of God. Using affirmations of life, I take the fear out of everyday living. My positive attitude imprints on my mind and within my body.

"For the kingdom of God is not food and drink
but righteousness and peace and joy in the Holy Spirit."
—Romans 14:17

Rx for Prayer

By Mel Richardson, M.D.

T he most empowering thing any of us can do is to let go and let God meet all our needs. This is how we draw upon the spiritual side of us, and that's what I try to do. I know I am at my best when I let Spirit work through me.

As the medical director of an outpatient surgery center, I find that a smile or a touch, a comforting word or a prayer can go a long way in making the surgery experience better—not only for the patient but also for the attending doctors, nurses, and technicians.

In the pre-op area, I prepare people for surgery. Because of the medical and legal aspects of practicing medicine today, I am required to tell people about the risks and potential complications of surgery and anesthesia. But I feel it is even more important to make a heart connection with my patients and allay their anxieties about having surgery.

Fear contributes to a patient's difficulty after surgery; it's counterproductive to the surgery itself. For example, many patients who are having a biopsy are afraid that the doctor will find cancer—their apprehension is visible. But as I pray with them and talk with them, they relax and become peaceful. I hold their hands, rub their temples, and reassure them as I prepare them for surgery.

I tell them that they're going to wake up and feel as if they've had the best sleep ever, that they won't experience pain or nausea. Such suggestions seem to help diminish nausea following surgery and lessen the amount of medication that the patient requires post-operatively.

Often patients will request prayer prior to going into the operating room, so I pray with them. Usually I have some type of relaxing music playing—whatever might help comfort or quiet them as they are going to sleep.

Studies have actually shown that surgery goes better when music is played in the operating room. The whole surgical team becomes involved, and surgeons as well as nurses comfort the patients as they go to sleep. During surgery, I often continue to whisper, "You're doing fine," for I know positive encouragement reaches them and helps stabilize them.

I work a lot with children—usually for some short procedure such as a tonsillectomy. The children are not quite as apprehensive as their parents. So working with the parents is important because children pick up on the anxiety of their parents, making the pre-operative procedures more difficult. When the parents are able to let go and let God, the children do much better.

I use different techniques with kids. I blow up a surgical glove and draw a picture, a funny face, and their names. That usually breaks the ice. I also have them pick a flavor of mask in the operating room. Whatever flavor they choose—strawberry, bubble gum, banana, cherry—is the flavor they smell as they're going off to sleep rather than the anesthetic gas smell. These are things that make the experience of going into the operating room and having a mask put over their faces easier. They feel they are a part of the surgical experience, that they have some control over what happens to them.

I'm not the only doctor who does these kinds of things in the operating room. But as a doctor I know that I need to do more than minister to my patients on a physical level; I need to minister to them on a spiritual level also.

This is the message that keeps coming to me as I care for people. Spirit speaks to me through patients, my wife, articles in publications, and different physicians concerning the spiritual care of the patient.

Prayer keeps me attuned to and listening for spiritual guidance. This is why prayer is so incredibly important in my work as a physician.

Peace of Mind

———◆———

*God gives me peace of mind
and comforts my heart.*

In a small boat on a stormy sea, a group of men huddled together in fear. Water was rising in the boat as it was tossed about by raging waves. Finally, in desperation, they turned to Jesus, who was sleeping in the stern. "He woke up and rebuked the wind, and said to the sea, 'Peace! Be still!' Then the wind ceased, and there was a dead calm" (Mark 4:39).

In the midst of my own stormy thoughts or emotions, I, too, may feel despair. Yet I, too, can find a place of peace by repeating Jesus' powerful words: "Peace! Be still!"

The peace of God calms all fear. As divine peace washes over me, my mind and heart are soothed. I know without a doubt that wherever I am, God is watching over me and restoring my inner peace.

> "He woke up and rebuked the wind, and said
> to the sea, 'Peace! Be still!' Then the wind ceased,
> and there was a dead calm."
> —Mark 4:39

God's Will

———◆———

Being open to the will of God prepares me to recognize and accept my blessings.

Do I ever resist something that is for my own good? I try not to do that. As the Psalmist did, I pray to be open and nonresistant to all blessings: "I delight to do your will, O my God; your law is within my heart" (Psalms 40:8).

When I get my own will—which at its best is still formed by my limited understanding—out of the way, I see a world of opportunity before me. I do not resist having to stretch and grow beyond my current capabilities. In the process of doing more and being more, I discover new talents and strengths and a zest for life.

My delight is in doing the will of God. When I flow along with the happenings of the day, I cooperate with the unfolding of blessings that bring a spark of joy and thanksgiving to my life and the lives of others.

> "Your kingdom come.
> Your will be done,
> on earth as it is in heaven."
> —Matthew 6:10

Healthy and Whole

———— ◆ ————

*I am healthy, whole,
and vitally alive!*

As I draw in a deep, satisfying breath, I marvel at how
my mind, heart, and lungs all work in perfect harmony
so that each breath comes easily for me.

I thank God for life. If at any time I am feeling less
than whole and healthy, I pray. I affirm that being vitally
alive is my true nature. At all times, the revitalizing spirit
of God is flowing throughout my body, healing me and
imbuing me with life.

In a sacred atmosphere of prayer, I am renewed. Each
time I give thanks for the complicated tasks my body
performs, I am enhancing my own well-being.

My body responds to the words of life and vitality
that I think and speak. I am healthy, whole, and vitally
alive!

> "Jesus said to him, 'Go; your faith has made
> you well.' Immediately he regained his sight
> and followed him on the way."
> —Mark 10:52

Divine Order

———◆———

*Divine order is God's
gracious gift to me.*

I cannot see the wind, but I can see its power in
swaying trees and high-flying kites. A refreshing breeze
on a warm day is a gentle reminder of the order of God
that is always present in my life, even if I cannot see it.

As with the wind, the invisibility of divine order takes
nothing away from its power. I may not be able to see
the divine order that is present all around me, but I
know that it is working mightily on my behalf.

Divine order is always present, always active. So in
spite of what may appear to be an absence of order, I
know it is there and trust God to do what is best. I may
not always understand the *why* and *how* of things, but I
can be sure of something else: Divine order is God's
gracious gift to me.

"Ever since the creation of the world,
his eternal power and divine nature, invisible
though they are, have been understood
and seen through the things he has made."
—Romans 1:20

I Believe!

——◆——

*I believe in the miracles of God because
I believe in God!*

Miracles are the unmistakable movement of the spirit of God in and through people and events. Miracles are affirmations of God's life, love, and power that all who are willing will see and hear and understand.

I am willing! I believe in the miracle-working power of God, for I see it every day. New life entering the world is a joyous proclamation of the wonder that God has created. The orderly way in which nature provides for all living creatures is according to a divine plan.

I believe in miracles, for I am a miracle in motion! How miraculous it is that my fingers bend and pick up objects and that my eyes see the twinkling light of stars which are trillions of miles away. Yes, I believe in the miracles of God because I believe in God!

> "He works signs and wonders
> in heaven and on earth."
> —Daniel 6:27

On Wings of Faith

——◆——

*On wings of faith, I soar
with spiritual freedom.*

The emergence of a butterfly from its cocoon is an awesome event. Yet before the butterfly can emerge, it is necessary for it to go through a transformation—a time of growth and change, rest and preparation for the new creation it will become. Then, on wings of faith, the butterfly soars into the air with greater freedom than it ever had before, fulfilling its divine purpose and potential.

I, too, may go through changes that affect me physically and emotionally. Yet no matter how many changes I go through, one thing remains the same—the spirit of God is within me. It is Spirit that sets me free to reach new heights of health and wholeness.

On wings of faith, I recognize my spiritual freedom and allow God's love to lift me to greater and greater heights.

"Now the Lord is the Spirit, and where the Spirit
of the Lord is, there is freedom."
—2 Corinthians 3:17

Spiritual Quest

—◆—

*Thank You, God, for leading me through
the adventures of my life.*

Thank God I do not have to climb a mountain to feel
the exhilaration a mountaintop experience brings.
Without taking a single physical step, I have embarked
on a spiritual quest that continues to enrich me.

I am on a spiritual quest in which I live as a sacred
being! This is a journey of the soul in which I discover
more about God and about the presence and power of
God in me. Not content to merely exist, I eagerly
explore my world, learning and growing through the
experiences of life.

Yes, I am on a journey of discovery! Each day I
welcome opportunities to discover the newness of life.
And each day I expand my understanding of what God
can do through me. With a grateful heart I say, "Thank
You, God, for life!"

> "'I am the Alpha and the Omega,'
> says the Lord God, who is and who was
> and who is to come, the Almighty."
> —Revelation 1:8

God Speaks to Me

—◆—

*God speaks to me, giving me guidance
and assurance along my way.*

There are many ways that God communicates with me,
so I remain alert and receptive to God's message for me.

When I ask God the questions on my heart, I may
receive answers in unexpected ways: An idea comes up
in a conversation with a friend or an inspirational
message is revealed as the lyrics of a song.

God also communicates with me in ways known
only to me. Although at first I may not be able to
explain *why* I feel so at peace in a time of crisis, I soon
understand that the gentle reassurance I am receiving is
because God is comforting me.

God may talk to me through a major event that
serves as a signpost that points me in the direction I
need to move. I watch and listen. Then I follow divine
guidance.

"God spoke to Israel in visions of the night."
—Genesis 46:2

Meditation

—◆—

*"Then the Lord God . . . breathed into
his nostrils the breath of life."*
—Genesis 2:7

As I become quiet, I concentrate on my breathing.
Aware of each breath, I fill my lungs with oxygen-
rich air, hold it for a few seconds, and then release
it. I take in fresh air and release all concern.

Breathing slowly and deeply, I feel any tension
in my body melt away. In its place there is a warm
glow as the cells of my body seem to awaken.

I continue to breathe and let the sacred silence
within my soul enfold me. The deeper my breaths
are, the more I feel the presence of God.

I am totally aware of God. Lingering in the
presence of God, I feel a complete satisfaction
within my soul.

Then, slowly, I again focus on my breathing. I
let each breath bring me further along in an
awareness of my surroundings.

Spending time in silence with God, I am
refreshed and ready for whatever this day holds in
store for me.

Prayer

—◆—

*"But the wisdom from above is first pure,
then peaceable, gentle, willing to yield,
full of mercy and good fruits."*
—James 3:17

In surrendering to You, God, I have nothing to lose and so much to gain. As I surrender my mind to Your wisdom, my heart to Your love, my life to Your healing presence, I am prepared to receive Your blessings.

Surrendering to You, God, can only be a victory for me. In sweet surrender, I am giving up worry for the peace of mind that Your presence brings me. I am eliminating stress that would interfere with the natural healing process of my body.

I know that whatever I give to You, God, will be healed and resolved. And I cooperate with Your desire to bless me by being open to the powerful, miraculous results that only You can bring about.

There is renewed life stirring within me. I feel as if the sun has come out after a long gray spell. Because I have surrendered all to You, all is indeed well. I am living in the light of Your presence.

Listen, Beloved

— ◆ —

Beloved,

I am with you always. My strength is your strength. Rest assured that I will guide you through every circumstance that may arise.

When you have done everything you can think of to find a solution to a challenge, stop *doing* and start *listening* to My message of love and assurance.

Your faith in Me is surpassed only by My faith in you, for I created you with your own unique qualities and the ability to overcome any challenge.

Yes, I am with you always, so never let yourself feel that you are alone in any challenge or achievement.

We are partners, beloved, and we are working together each day to create more love and faith in the world.

"Haggai, the messenger of the Lord,
spoke to the people with the Lord's message,
saying, 'I am with you, says the Lord.'"
—*Haggai 1:13*

Hero

——◆——

*God has made me a hero—a spiritual being
of invincible wisdom and power.*

Often it is only the people who have accomplished great feats, such as rescuing others, putting out forest fires, or discovering lifesaving vaccines, who are thought of as heroes.

I have cause to celebrate their victories and give thanks for their accomplishments. Yet I, too, have that heroic nature within me, and it is just waiting to be released. I am filled with the dynamic power and creative genius of God.

Whether in times of crisis or in everyday matters, I can call upon my faith in the spirit of God within me to help me rise above any challenge to my health or well-being.

Today and every day, I have cause to celebrate the hero that exists within me. God has given me all I need to be an invincible spiritual being of wisdom and power.

> **"Our mouth was filled with laughter,
> and our tongue with shouts of joy."**
> **—Psalms 126:2**

A Healthy Heart

——◆——

By praying life-affirming prayers, eating smart,
and exercising, I bless my heart.

I am thankful that my body sustains itself whether or not I am consciously aware of how or why it happens.

The constant, rhythmic beating of my heart is an amazing example. Even when I am at rest, my heart continues to pump oxygen-rich blood throughout my body—all without me having to tell it how to work.

I am proactive in maintaining a healthy heart when I eat nourishing foods and exercise. By eating smart and being active, I help to keep my arteries clear, which in turn allows the blood to move freely throughout my body.

I also keep my thoughts positive, relieving my heart of any undue stress. I remain relaxed and stress-free as I remain God-focused.

And I remember to say, "Thank You, God, for my strong, healthy heart!"

> "If we live by the Spirit, let us
> also be guided by the Spirit."
> —Galatians 5:25

Answering the Call

———◆———

*I answer the call to life and cooperate
with God's plan of abundant life.*

I never want to take any of God's creations for granted.
I have a deep, abiding reverence for my life and for
all life.

The call to life resounds everywhere in the
environment—season by season, year by year. A tiny
acorn that has been planted in the soil by an industrious
squirrel answers the call. The acorn is transformed into
a magnificent oak tree.

The same call to life is being answered by the blades
of grass breaking through the cracks of a sidewalk as
well as those breaking through the soil of a lawn. The
newborn whale rising to the surface of the sea for its
first breath is answering the call to life.

I, too, answer the call—to life and to do all that I can
to cooperate with God's plan of abundant life for me
and for the diverse life on planet Earth.

**"God called the dry land Earth, and the waters
that were gathered together he called Seas.
And God saw that it was good."
—Genesis 1:10**

Expression of Joy

—◆—

God, I am thankful to be a living,
breathing expression of Your joy.

For a moment, I imagine how I would feel being fully in
the presence of God: Oh, yes, I feel a joy rising from
within my soul and I experience a spiritual gladness
with every fiber of my being!

The absolutely beautiful and powerful truth is that I
am always in the presence of God. The spirit of God is
within me and permeates the atmosphere and people
and situations I am a part of in every moment of life.

So if, because of the appearance of illness, I am
feeling less than joyous, I remember that God is within
me as a source of joy of the soul and healing life that are
always waiting to be experienced and expressed by me.
I give thanks that the joy of God is such a comfort in
times of change and adjustment, such a boost to me in
times of fulfillment and accomplishment.

I am a living, breathing expression of the joy of God.

> "Be glad in the Lord and rejoice."
> —Psalms 32:11

Showers of Blessings

—◆—

God showers me with blessings.

Much like the thirsty earth absorbs the rain, so do I accept the showers of blessings that God is pouring out to me.

Just as the nourished earth gives birth to abundant, new life, so do I express a renewal of life. I think clearly as inspired ideas lead me to new discoveries. My understanding of myself and others grows and expands— nourishing my relationships.

There is an abundance of life that is stirring within me. I have the energy I need to act on the new opportunities that are revealed to me in times of prayer and reflection.

Today and every day, I give thanks to God for the abundance of blessings that are continually being showered upon me. I am revitalized!

> "Give ear, O heavens, and I will speak;
> let the earth hear the words of my mouth.
> May my teachings drop like the rain,
> my speech condense like the dew;
> like gentle rain on grass,
> like showers on new growth."
> —Deuteronomy 32:1–2

Masterpiece

——◆——

*I am a priceless masterpiece
of God's creation.*

What elevates one painting above another so that it is declared to be a work of art? Maybe that painting gives the beholder a glimpse into the soul of the one who painted it.

My own ideas about art are probably very different from those of my family and friends. Yet we may all agree on this: The love and inspiration that go into a creation are what make it a treasure of the heart.

God created me with love, and I let the love of God shine from me as brightly as priceless gems. I am a masterpiece of the Master Creator.

Truly, the presence of God within me is a treasure of eternal life and vitality. It is a treasure that is forever an integral part of me as a priceless work of God's creation.

**"Let your adornment be the inner self
with the lasting beauty of a gentle and quiet spirit,
which is very precious in God's sight."
—1 Peter 3:4**

Healthy Perception

———— ◆ ————

*I have a healthy perception that acknowledges
the presence of God in all and through all.*

If I am facing a healing challenge, I know that it's
important for me to have and to keep a healthy
perception of myself and my world. My body responds
to my thoughts of health and well-being.

A positive perception does make a difference. I help
myself and others by holding to life-affirming images
that acknowledge the presence of God in all people,
challenges, and changes. Instead of focusing on what I
perceive is wrong, I look for and find what is right and
good and true about us as creations of God.

My healthy perception of life serves as a catalyst for
renewed faith and hope in me and around me. I
understand that for every challenge, God has a solution.
I pray knowing that for every prayer, God has an
answer. Wherever there is a need, there is a fulfillment of
that need—all through the presence and power of God.

**"Truly I tell you, many prophets and righteous people
longed to see what you see, but did not see it, and to hear
what you hear, but did not hear it."
—Matthew 13:17**

Yes, I Can!

———◆———

Yes, God,
I can!

My spirit soars with the music as I listen to a composition of melody, harmony, and rhythm that builds to a glorious finish. I feel the creativity of God uplifting me as it is expressed by composers and musicians. Having been inspired, I am ready to say, "Yes, I can!" to accomplishing something.

Yes, I can overcome any situation that moments before seemed overwhelming. I have the power and strength of God's presence to guide and sustain me.

Yes, I can live whole and free—healthy in mind, body, and spirit. I was created for life, and I am fulfilling my divine destiny of wholeness.

Yes, I can do all things that God leads me to do, because God fills me with creative thoughts that show me all kinds of possibilities.

Yes, I can, because God is my inspiration, strength, and wisdom.

> **"I can do all things through him**
> **who strengthens me."**
> **—Philippians 4:13**

Meditation

—◆—

*"For thus said the Lord God, the Holy One
of Israel: 'In returning and rest you shall be saved;
in quietness and in trust shall be your strength.'"*
—Isaiah 30:15

When I become still and quiet my thoughts, I give
my whole self over to experiencing the presence
of God.

I envision myself as free and formless—not
constricted by physical shape or space. The spirit
of God within me unites me with the spirit of God
everywhere.

What power is released in this quiet time of
prayer! I am at ease and completely relaxed so that
there is a free flow of life and energy throughout
my body. I fairly tingle with life and vitality.

I linger in the quiet; here I know my oneness
with my Creator. When I come back to the activity
of the day, I am still glowing with an awareness of
God and I am filled with energy.

Prayer

"The Lord will guide you continually . . .
and you shall be like a watered garden,
like a spring of water, whose waters never fail."
—Isaiah 58:11

God, thank You for never giving up on me—even when I am ready to give up on myself. Your spirit within me gives me constant reassurance that there is a way through every crisis and new insight into every challenge.

I am willing to listen to You, God, and to learn from You. With that willingness, I open myself to Your guidance in everyday matters and in major events. Divine guidance lifts the cloud of concern. I am refreshed and free—ready to do what is mine to do.

God, Your guidance reveals the golden opportunities that are there for me. Now I see the wonder of You everywhere! I am moving forward—guided, loved, and inspired by You.

Listen, Beloved

—◆—

Beloved,

Begin now to open your heart and your life to the freedom I have already given you. As surely as you believe in Me, allow yourself to believe that you are free—free with the freedom of My spirit within you.

Freedom is your inheritance from Me. I created you to be free—free to think and act from My spirit within you; free to live with an enthusiasm for life that lights up the very atmosphere wherever you are; free to love unconditionally and compassionately, faithfully and eternally.

There is no person who can keep you from expressing your freedom of spirit. There is nothing that can hold you back from being the loving person I created you to be.

You are free—free and healed of all wounds from the past. You are free to enjoy life now.

Yes, beloved, you are free.

"When Jesus saw her, he called her over and said,
'Woman, you are set free from your ailment.'"
—Luke 13:12

Uplifted Soul

——◆——

God, You alone
uplift my soul.

In a peaceful time of prayer, my soul is uplifted by the presence of God. I am inspired by the wisdom of God as it penetrates to my most hidden thoughts. Then I am able to release all concern and any urgency to force a solution to a problem.

My soul is uplifted, and I feel at peace about this day and the days ahead. I relax and revel in the warm glow of peace that comes from being in the presence of God. Here with God, I know that there is nothing to fear.

With tenderness and love, God shows me the way around or through a challenge. Although God may show me more than one path, the one I take is up to me. As I move forward, I am blessed all along my way by the love and understanding, encouragement and support of God.

> "Teach me the way I should go,
> for to you I lift up my soul."
> —Psalms 143:8

The Answer

—◆—

God is the answer
to every healing need.

The promise of spring lies underneath the barren soil of winter. Such a promise is a reminder of the healing, renewing power of God that is within me.

My own need for healing may go beyond the physical and what can be seen on the outside. Perhaps I am in a relationship that needs the healing love of forgiveness. Or maybe I need to be healed of emotional pain that has become a real challenge to my peace of mind.

Whatever the healing need is, God is the answer. The spirit of God within me is life that nourishes, heals, and renews me.

The spirit of God soothes my mind and body. My needs are met and I am healed and whole.

> "O Lord my God, I cried to you for help,
> and you have healed me."
> —Psalms 30:2

Graduate

—◆—

*Today is my graduation day, because I
am moving on to greater wisdom.*

Probably the biggest defeat I can give to my spiritual
awareness and my emotional well-being is to berate
myself for not doing something better or differently.
The reality of life is that I always have much more to
learn—no matter what my age or experiences may be. I
am always learning!

Life is often compared to a school of learning. At
times, I may learn more from mistakes than from
accomplishments. If I make a mistake, I remind myself
that I can do better and that I did the best I could at
the time.

I am a student in life, and I have a divine instructor.
So as I move on with my life, I graduate from one level
of understanding to a higher level. I gain wisdom that
prepares me for a full and fulfilling life.

"The drippings of the honeycomb are sweet
to your taste. Know that wisdom is such
to your soul."
—Proverbs 24:13–14

Healing Response

—◆—

*A powerful healing response of my immune system
is constantly taking place within me.*

My immune system doesn't need me to tell it to go on
the defense and neutralize bacteria or viruses; it does
this according to a divine plan.

Yet I do believe my life-affirming thoughts and
prayers stimulate my immune system. I know there is
intelligence within my immune system that responds to
my words of life and healing.

Antibodies know to be selective as they rush to
prevent an invasion against my health and well-being.
These antibodies have a memory that prompts an
immediate response so that I am immune to that kind
of threat—even for a lifetime.

My positive attitude supports the healing of my
body. It's as if my words of life encourage my immune
system to do what it does best: keep my body as pure
and whole as it was created to be.

I am healthy, strong, and vibrantly alive!

> "Then your light shall break forth like the dawn,
> and your healing shall spring up quickly."
> —Isaiah 58:8

Feeling Confident

———◆———

*Thank You, God, for the confidence I receive
from Your understanding, love, and peace.*

Feeling confident about the decisions I have made and
my ability to accomplish goals does not guarantee that I
will live a life free of doubt. I may still experience times
of uncertainty.

Yet I will never allow doubt to limit me or what I can
accomplish when I rely on God. In every situation, I
invite the light of divine understanding to shine in my
decisions and actions.

The love of God comforts and soothes me. I have the
strength and courage to keep on keeping on. Like the
sunlight breaking through the clouds, the warmth of
God's love shines within me and upon me.

Softly, tenderly, God assures me—dispelling all doubt
and hesitation. I am enfolded in the peace of God.

> "He who has prepared us for this very thing
> is God, who has given us the Spirit as a guarantee.
> So we are always confident."
> —2 Corinthians 5:5–6

Garden of Life

——◆——

*My life is a garden that is nourished
and cared for by God.*

My life is much like a garden that goes through amazing
changes from season to season. Yet such changes
introduce a rich variety of experiences, people, and
growth that remind me of how truly blessed I am.

Like a beautiful garden reaching toward the light for
its full potential, I thrive. I have had and continue to
receive nourishment and care. God creates and provides
all that I need for continued growth and fulfillment.

God sustains me and is my constant companion,
walking with me in the garden of life. I am encouraged
as I see the beauty and wonder that are there and I
visualize the great potential for blessings yet to be.

"They shall flourish as a garden;
they shall blossom like the vine,
their fragrance shall be like the wine of Lebanon."
—Hosea 14:7

TODAY'S MESSAGE:
Creating a New Me

—◆—

*Through healthy eating and a sensible exercise plan,
I am creating a new me!*

I've probably never thought that following a specific diet could be a pleasant experience, but it can be when I make a shift in my thinking. Rather than dwelling on what I have to give up, I now think about all the things I will gain by changing my lifestyle and eating habits.

One of the most immediate benefits is that I am taking responsibility for my own well-being. I am helping my heart to work more efficiently and my body to function more effectively.

I also gain a better self-image, a sense of all that is possible for the new me I am creating. And what a sense of achievement I have when I begin to see the results of my work! If I can do this, I can do anything!

Yes, I will have to discipline myself, but I do so knowing that God is the strength I need to create the new me!

> "Be glad and rejoice forever
> in what I am creating."
> —Isaiah 65:18

Expectations

—◆—

*Thank You, God, for blessing me in ways
that are greater even than my highest expectations.*

I am so thankful that God does not limit my blessings
to only my expectations or the expectations of others.

At one time, I thought I was giving all the love I was
capable of giving, but my heart yearned to love more.
Then God sent someone who caused love to surge from
my heart. I learned that because God loves through me,
I always have more love to give.

Just when I thought I had done all I could do to move
past a negative habit, God told me, "Give any concern
or fear of failure to Me, and I will give you the strength
and power to overcome." And God did that.

I never want to limit my expectations of God's
blessings, and I am thankful that divine blessings
surpass my highest expectations. I thank God for
blessing me with life, health, love, and understanding.

> **"For God alone my soul waits in silence,
> for my hope is from him."
> —Psalms 62:5**

THE WONDERFUL GIFT OF LIFE

BY KAROLYN (ZUZU) GRIMES

The Christmas tree on the set for the film *It's a Wonderful Life* was the most beautiful one I had ever seen. Almost touching the ceiling of the Bailey's Victorian parlor, the tree sparkled with miniature angels and bells.

I was a 6-year-old actress, and for a few months I was going to be a member of the Bailey family. In real life, I was an only child and lonely. While making the movie, I would have a brother and sisters to play with and a gentle, loving man as my father.

Jimmy Stewart brought his patience and love for children to the set of the classic 1946 movie. In one scene, we were coming down a flight of stairs. His arms were full carrying two other children, and I was hanging from Jimmy's back with my arms wrapped about his neck, literally choking him. The scene had to be shot over and over again, but Jimmy never lost patience with me or the other children. He was always kind and generous.

I was in more than 16 movies before the age of 15, but being Zuzu, a member of the Bailey family, blessed me for the rest of my life. I learned that a family is about love and acceptance. Even today I regard those who played the Bailey children as my real brother and sisters. And over the years, Jimmy Stewart and I became true friends.

Life took a sudden turn when I was a teenager. My mother, who had been very ill for years, died when I was 14. My father was killed in an automobile accident when I was 15. I moved from California to the Midwest to live with the only family I had: my father's brother and his wife.

My career as an actress was not only over, it was something that was not even to be discussed in my new home. Like my movie memorabilia that were stored in a trunk in a dark corner of a shed, my memories were pushed back into a dark corner of my mind.

I married young just to get out of the mentally abusive atmosphere of that house, and the marriage lasted only a few years. During those few years, however, two beautiful daughters were born.

In order for me to make enough money to support myself and my children, we moved from the small town where we had lived to a large city. Later I met and married a man who had three children of his own. We were married for 25 years and had two more children. Together we had a total of seven children!

God gave me the tools and the strength to cope with the loss of one of our sons. When John committed suicide at age 18, it took years to rebuild our lives, yet his death drew our family closer together. We turned to each other and held together in ways that we never would have otherwise.

John left his family and friends a legacy of love. He had told us that his best friend's family didn't have much money, and when we walked into this family's home, where John was found, there was no heat. Because of him, we were inspired to reach out and help others through our own lives and through a fund that gives boys an opportunity for an education that they might not otherwise have. John's best friend was one who was helped by the fund, and he is now a lawyer who contributes greatly to his community.

We each touch the lives of other people. As we live our lives each day, we make choices that touch others in powerful and meaningful ways. God gives us the freedom to make our choices and to make them lovingly and compassionately—as God's family.

I have a second career now—not in the movies, but because of the movie *It's a Wonderful Life*. The movie that was a flop in 1946 became a hit in the 1970s, and I started receiving fan mail in the 1980s.

The fan mail continued to escalate, and now the Zuzu Society has more than 3,000 members! I travel throughout the United States speaking and signing autographs. I talk to organizations and bereavement groups. People tell me their stories and that they watch *It's a*

Wonderful Life year-round. When they are depressed or feel down, the uplifting message of the movie seems to heal their spirits and give them hope.

I believe that's true for many people. Jimmy Stewart plays George Bailey, a banker facing financial ruin and wishing he had never been born. Then an angel named Clarence appears and shows George how the lives of others would not have been so blessed had he not been born and how his presence would be missed in the future.

My favorite scene in the film is when George is standing on the bridge. He realizes what he truly values is not anything tangible. What is important are his family, friends, and the love they share. He puts his hands to his face and says: "I want to live again. Dear God, I want to live again!" Then the snow starts falling. When George finds the petals of a rose that Zuzu had given him in his pocket, he knows he is back living life again.

Like George Bailey, let's know that life is a wonderful gift and that we each touch the lives of others and make a difference. Sometimes just smiling at people can make their day or give them hope. God has given us the gift of life, so let's discover and enjoy just how wonderful life is. By giving of ourselves, we can also be like the angel Clarence, helping each other to know that the world would not be the same without each one of us.

God's Word

———◆———

God's word is a sacred trust
that I rely on today and every day.

Oh, what a sacred trust a promise is! It's a commitment by the one who made the promise to never let anyone or anything get in the way of the fulfillment of the good that is desired.

The word of God is a promise that I can rely on in every moment of my life: "Thus says the Lord . . . 'I will make an everlasting covenant with them, never to draw back from doing good to them' " (Jeremiah 32:36,40).

I know that God fulfills this promise by constantly blessing me with life and sustaining me in life. God's promise includes the presence of good in every situation—even though I may not be able to perceive it. So I put worries aside and trust God to see me through all circumstances.

> "His divine power has given us everything needed
> for life and godliness, through the knowledge
> of him who called us by his own glory and goodness.
> Thus he has given us, through these things,
> his precious and very great promises."
> —2 Peter 1:3–4

Divine Assurance

———◆———

*My awareness of God is a powerful assurance
that makes my life complete!*

I feel a powerful assurance to the core of my being
when I think of what is true about me: God is an
integral part of me and my life. This assurance sets off a
rejoicing within my soul that could never be equaled by
anything happening outside of me.

I am filled with an awareness of God! I experience an
uplifting of my soul that comes from this awareness.
No other experience can equal the experience of
knowing that God is my healer and my companion.

Life is for living, and I live life with enthusiasm! Every
breath I take is cause for celebration. I am grateful for
life and even more thankful that the Creator of all that is
known and unknown loves and cares for me.

> "I have said these things to you so that
> my joy may be in you, and that your joy
> may be complete."
> —John 15:11

Discovery

— ◆ —

*I am discovering the wonder of God within me
and within all life.*

I can never exhaust my desire to discover the wonder
that God has created. I take it all in through my
senses—the vast array of scenes, the sounds and
fragrances, the tastes and textures.

I do not, however, let all the wonder around me keep
me from discovering the wonder that is within me. I am
an amazing creation of the Creator. To discover my true
identity, I search within my own soul.

There is more to me than form, shape, and substance.
What can be seen on the outside is marvelous, but it is
only a hint of the magnificence that is within. In the
sanctuary of my soul, the spiritual me resides.

I am an eternal, spiritual being, experiencing life and
discovering more of the wonder of God in me and in
all life.

"The heavens are telling the glory of God;
and the firmament proclaims his handiwork."
—Psalms 19:1

Sweet Surrender

——◆——

In sweet surrender, I invite God to work marvels in and through me.

I may be quicker at releasing some negative experiences than others. I feel no reluctance in letting go of the hot handle of a pan, yet for my own well-being I also need to remember to let go of worrisome thoughts. What I do after I have let them go is even more important: I give God my full attention.

This is both a practical and powerful way of sustaining emotional and physical well-being. When I give a concern to God, I am saying, "Here I am, God, and here is a situation out of which I know You can work a miracle."

What immediate relief I feel with this sweet surrender! The energy I had been directing toward a problem is regained as strength that is directed toward following a divine plan. I recognize God as God and also acknowledge that God is working marvels in and through me.

> "But surely, God is my helper;
> the Lord is the upholder of my life."
> —Psalms 54:4

I Am Renewed

——◆——

In prayer, the peace of God sweeps
over my soul, and I am renewed.

Some mornings, just getting out of bed and handling
the routine of the day can be a challenge. A hectic
schedule can leave me feeling drained of energy and
strength. Responsibilities at work and home may have
me wondering how much more I can possibly do.

Making changes in my schedule and in my life may
not be the only answer. The peace I discover in even a
brief time of prayer brings me immediate relief. So I go
to God in prayer. In a quiet time of communion with
God, I feel the presence of God and a peace that sweeps
over my soul to renew and restore me.

Along with this renewal comes a resurgence of the
energy I need to do all that is mine to do today and to
do it well. At peace within myself, I begin anew.

"I pray that, according to the riches of his glory,
he may grant that you may be strengthened in your
inner being with power through his Spirit."
—Ephesians 3:16

Motivated

— ◆ —

*The spirit of God within motivates me
to do my best.*

I may be such a peaceful and assured person that other people ask what motivates me to be this way. If this question should come up, I know that my answer will be this: The spirit of God within me motivates me to do my best.

I have faith in God. Just as important, God has faith in me. Divinely inspired ideas that seem to just pop into my mind are messages of encouragement from God. My Creator is telling me I have the ability to carry through on the guidance I receive—whether that guidance is to improve my health by walking for 30 minutes several times a week or to improve my finances by trying out for a promotion.

Knowing that God has faith in me, I am motivated to do my best. I go about doing my best with an enthusiasm for life!

> "I am sending him to you for this very purpose,
> to let you know how we are,
> and to encourage your hearts."
> —Ephesians 6:22

Healing the World

——◆——

*In caring for children, I am helping
to heal the world.*

Every investment in a child is an investment in the
future of the world. Whether I give love, guidance, and
tender care to my own children or to other children in a
role as parent, teacher, neighbor, or friend, I can help to
heal the world.

In caring about and for children, I allow the love of
God to move through me. The frightened child I
comfort today may become the future astronaut who
explores the universe. This is possible because I have
helped a child know that we can never stray beyond
God's love and care.

The child I take by the hand and guide today may be
a pathfinder to a world at peace tomorrow. All children
who share a vision of the sacred kinship we have with
every other person on planet Earth will desire to be
peacemakers. Then the world will be healed.

"Every generous act of giving, with every perfect gift,
is from above, coming down from the Father of lights."
—James 1:17

Flow of Life

———◆———

*Because I am a living, loving creation of God, there is
a constant flow of divine life throughout my body.*

How humbling yet exhilarating it is for me to realize
that I am just one of the wonders of life in a world full
of God's wonders. Divine life flowing throughout all
creation is also flowing through me.

The evidence of God's creativity is everywhere: The
rising sun each morning warms me with golden rays
and lights my way; the leaves on the trees produce fresh
oxygen for me to breathe. There is divine order in the
world, and a divine flow of life throughout the world.

Life pulsates throughout my body, which is a
magnificent machine created to sustain the gift of life. I
care for and nurture my body by eating healthy food
and exercising regularly.

Divine life flows through me now because I am a
living, loving creation of God.

"The earth produces of itself, first the stalk,
then the head, then the full grain in the head."
—Mark 4:28

Meditation

—◆—

*"And forgive us our debts, as we also
have forgiven our debtors."—Matthew 6:12*

In a solitary place where nothing can distract me, I
ask God to help me forgive. I may never before
have considered that forgiveness is a way I can
help myself to heal emotionally and physically. In
this quiet time, God assures me that as I forgive, I
will heal.

My response to God is, "Yes, God, I will
forgive; I will be healed." I speak the words, "I
forgive myself for anything hurtful or harmful I
have done." Even if I am unable to speak to
someone in person, I say, "I forgive you for
anything hurtful or harmful you have done." Then
I feel the blessed relief that forgiveness brings.

God has helped me to give the forgiveness I
could not bring myself to give. Forgiving myself and
others is something that heals me emotionally. The
relief from emotional stress allows a free flow of
healing energy throughout my body. I am healed.

From God's love within me, I do forgive. I
release the painful memories, and I am ready to
rebuild old relationships and to build new ones.

Prayer

— ◆ —

"Do not let the sun go down on your anger."
—Ephesians 4:26

God, when I feel okay physically yet lack the energy or initiative to be supportive, productive, or creative, I wonder what is the matter with me. Then You remind me that it could be that I am carrying an emotional burden of fear, regret, or resentment that a heartfelt prayer can relieve.

You help me to help myself through forgiveness, God. I may not remember whom or what it is I need to forgive, so I allow Your love and understanding to relieve me of any negative thoughts and emotions.

I forgive myself for things I may have done or left undone. I forgive others for what they have done to me or said about me.

I don't let myself go through one day carrying a burden that forgiveness will relieve. For those people and experiences that seem beyond my capacity to forgive, I allow Your spirit of unconditional love within me to be expressed by me as forgiveness.

DAILY WORD FOR HEALING

Listen, Beloved

—◆—

Beloved,

I love you with a love that upholds you and never condemns you.

Forgive yourself for what you call mistakes. They were times when you were brave enough to allow yourself to learn and grow.

Let My peace fill your soul and allow My love to guide your way and inspire your thoughts and words.

Permit yourself to fully grasp the magnitude of My love for all that I have created. Forgive others. Put aside any tendency to judge them and then let My serenity fill the void.

I am absolute peace. I am unconditional love. My love for you is eternal.

With My love supporting you, you will forgive yourself and others and heal your relationships with one another. Then you shall live in peace.

"Render to all whose heart you know,
according to all their ways, for only
you know the human heart."
—2 Chronicles 6:30

Joy of Laughter

——◆——

*My laughter is a rejoicing
of my body and soul.*

It has been said that God is the author of laughter. I believe this because I feel the joy of God fully awakening my body each time I laugh.

I feel alive—full to the brim with joy—when I let go with a hearty laugh. Joy speaks to my heart and encourages it to beat in a steady, strong rhythm. The joy of laughter dissipates any anxiety and sends forth a rush of peace that causes my whole body to relax.

Oh, how good it is to share my laughter with others! Joy vibrates from within me and announces that I am giving expression to the gladness within my soul. This is the kind of laughter that uplifts the spirits of all who hear it and express it.

My laughter is a celebration of the spirit of God within me, spilling out from me as a rejoicing of body and soul.

**"The joy of the Lord is your strength."
—Nehemiah 8:10**

TODAY'S MESSAGE:
Affirm Health

— ◆ —

*Now and throughout the day,
I affirm my health and wholeness.*

Whether I am feeling on top of the world or as if I need a little boost, I affirm my health and wholeness now and throughout the day.

There is amazing power in thinking and speaking positive, heartfelt words of life. Life-affirming thoughts and words resonate within my soul and stimulate the cells of my body. Cell by cell, my strength and vitality are enhanced. I feel the health and wholeness that I have been affirming.

My affirmations need not be lengthy or complicated in order to be effective. They need only be positive, life-affirming statements that confirm the power and presence of God's spirit within me.

Every life-affirming word I speak and thought I think promotes healing. My body says *yes* to the health and wholeness I have been affirming.

"Above all, my beloved, . . . let your 'Yes' be yes
and your 'No' be no."
—James 5:12

Vacation

—◆—

*In silence with God, I am refreshed
and renewed.*

A vacation can be a time of both physical rest and mental renewal. It is a chance to get away from the everyday routine and visit with friends and family.

Even when I cannot take time off from my job or responsibilities, however, I can still turn within to the quiet of my soul. Relaxing in silence, I can take a minivacation at any time. By stilling my thoughts and turning to the spirit of God within, I find relief from the busyness of the day and travel to a place of peace.

The presence of God awaits within my soul. Here I experience God's presence without interference from anything or anyone. I relax and unwind.

After spending just a few moments with God, I am refreshed. I come away rested and ready to enjoy the gift that each moment is.

**"I am with you always."
—Matthew 28:20**

Celebration!

— ◆ —

*I celebrate life and my divine freedom
to live life fully!*

Life is so full of blessings that I might take some—such as health, joy, or loved ones—for granted. Holidays and birthdays are great reminders to celebrate the gift of life. But each day is special.

Today, I celebrate life and the spiritual freedom God has created me to express. This is a new day in which God offers me diverse opportunities to learn and to grow.

My celebrations may be quiet, individual times of reflection or busy, active times with loved ones. Yet each celebration is in honor of the spiritual nature within.

With each thought, word, or action that honors the spirit of God within myself and others, I am celebrating the presence of God. What better reason is there for me to celebrate?

"We will go with our young and our old; we will go with our sons and daughters and with our flocks and herds, because we have the Lord's festival to celebrate."
—Exodus 10:9

Kingdom of God

———◆———

My body is a temple of the spirit of God.

If ever I have doubt about my healing, I remember these words Paul wrote to the Corinthians: "Do you not know that you are God's temple and that God's Spirit dwells in you? . . . God's temple is holy, and you are that temple" (1 Corinthians 3:16–17).

Knowing who I am, a holy temple of God, I realize all of the kingdom of God that is available to me. Health is one example. Whenever I pray about my health and well-being, I am claiming my inheritance from the kingdom of God: a healthy body and an active mind that reflect the spirit of God within me.

I cooperate with God by letting go of negative habits and accepting the good that God has for me. A divine plan unfolds as the spirit of God moves through me, building my body—an extraordinary temple—from the inside out.

> **"Then the King will say to those at his right hand,
> 'Come, you that are blessed by my Father,
> inherit the kingdom prepared for you from
> the foundation of the world.'"
> —Matthew 25:34**

Grace

—◆—

*Through the grace of God, I experience
the fullness of life.*

In my heart and mind I know that the thoughts I think
help shape my experiences in life. So as I think positive,
peace-filled thoughts, I open myself to the good that is
always there. Through the grace of God, I am given a
way around and over any obstacle.

Acknowledging that the grace of God is blessing me,
I feel new strength and courage rising within me. I can
and do overcome any challenge—mental or physical—
that could keep good from me. Because of God's grace,
my life is filled with abundant blessings.

No matter what the challenge may be, I am lifted and
carried along on the wings of God's love. I am sheltered
in the grace of God as I experience the fullness of life.

"Everything is for your sake, so that grace,
as it extends to more and more people,
may increase thanksgiving, to the glory of God."
—2 Corinthians 4:15

Blessed Journey

—◆—

*I give expression to the greatness, love,
and wisdom of God on my journey of life.*

My life is an unfolding journey of discovery, and I am
continually learning more about myself and awakening
to my spiritual identity.

I am enriched by experiencing many different
situations and opportunities. Whether I have reached
the peak of success or I am still down in a valley
traveling toward my goal, I give thanks for the blessings
that are being revealed to me.

Whenever I feel as if I am struggling in the darkness
of doubt, I remind myself that even the darkest night
soon gives way to the healing light of a new dawn. Life
experiences can be a proving ground that brings out the
strength of my spirituality. I am learning more and more
what I am capable of achieving as God expresses
greatness, love, and wisdom through me.

> **"Great and amazing are your deeds,
> Lord God the Almighty!"
> —Revelation 15:3**

Rebuilding

—◆—

*My faith-filled prayers promote healing
and restoration.*

Even a short-term health challenge can leave me feeling
less than capable of performing my normal daily tasks.
After I have recovered enough to resume my normal
activities, I may still feel as if I am not completely up to
par. At such times, I recognize that I am in the process
of healing and that I need to allow my body enough
time to heal.

So I take one day at a time, easing back into my
routine slowly and at a pace that does not cause more
strain. I do not force my body into activities that it is
not yet ready to perform. Instead, I let my strength
rebuild from the inside out and know that God is giving
me the energy I need to make progress.

I pray throughout the rebuilding process. Each prayer
reinforces my faith and renews my mind and body—
helping me to heal and regain my strength.

"I will set my eyes upon them for good. . . . I will build
them up, and not tear them down; I will plant them,
and not pluck them up. I will give them a heart to know
that I am the Lord."—Jeremiah 24:6–7

Meditation

— ◆ —

*"Ask, and it will be given you; search,
and you will find; knock, and the door
will be opened for you."*
—Matthew 7:7

I prepare for travel or for other activities so that I
am ready for the event. I also prepare myself
mentally for the outcome of an event—such as the
result of a medical test. My preparation is turning
within to God so that I am uplifted in spirit.

As I close my eyes and enter into a sacred time
of prayer, I picture myself surrounded by the
healing light of God. I see myself as God sees
me—whole, well, and free of all limitations.

I then envision myself receiving news about
those medical tests. Knowing that I am capable of
handling any type of results and that I am secure in
the knowledge that God is with me, I see a look of
confidence on my face. I feel a wave of peace that
soothes my soul.

I am prepared for any outcome, for my faith in
God is strong. God and I are one; with God, I face
the future with strength of mind, body, and spirit.

DAILY WORD FOR HEALING

Prayer

—◆—

"For God all things are possible."
—Matthew 19:26

God, when I am feeling stressed, I know that You
are my relief and my support.

Yet there may be times when I am so caught
up in concern about my health that I become filled
with doubt and anxieties about my ability to cope.
Then, oh, so gently, You remind me of Your loving
presence through a sudden feeling of peace that
permeates my entire being.

When I rely on You to guide me, God, I feel an
immediate ease from tension and stress because I
know that You will show me how to deal with any
problem that might come my way. We are
partners, God, and as I work with You and follow
Your inspiration, I realize that nothing is impossible
for me.

Thank You, God, for Your loving presence
within me and within every moment of my life.

Listen, Beloved

—◆—

Beloved,

You are whole and complete, no matter what appearances may be.

Look past the things you see in yourself as imperfections to the perfection that is My presence within you. Because I am life and love within you, you are whole and complete.

Your appearance is changing, and sometimes that might happen suddenly, but you are forever the essence of beauty and perfection to Me.

I know what you have been through, because I was with you all the way. Even during your most difficult time, the brilliance of your spirit was dazzling.

You have come a long way, and you still have far to go. Whenever you become weary, I will renew you with strength. Whenever you become downhearted, My love will revive you.

You, beloved, are whole and complete.

"I will greatly rejoice in the Lord,
my whole being shall exult in my God."
—*Isaiah 61:10*

Healthy and Fulfilled

——◆——

*I am healthy and fulfilled—a living expression
of the spirit of God within.*

I may become concerned about my own health after
reading or hearing about symptoms of an illness. Yet I
can put such thoughts aside and concentrate on living a
healthy, fulfilling life when I remember Jesus' inspiring
words: "Do not worry about your life, what you will
eat, or about your body, what you will wear. For life is
more than food, and the body more than clothing"
(Luke 12:22–23).

Yes, life is more—so much more than I can
personally see or feel at any one time. Life is for living
now, in this moment, and for giving wholehearted
expression to the spirit of God within.

God's spirit is the source of all healing and strength.
As I focus on the spirit of God within me, I feel alive
with divine life. Then I am as I was created to be—a
living expression of God's spirit within.

> **"I will restore health to you,
> and your wounds I will heal."
> —Jeremiah 30:17**

Gentle Touch

— ◆ —

*The invisible spirit of God takes on visibility
in the love of a caregiver.*

The loving, gentle touch of a caregiver is conveyed in many ways: as someone to lean on to steady people as they walk, as someone to listen as others release their pent-up concerns.

The love of God within every caregiver—parent, child, doctor, nurse, teacher, and friend—reaches out in soothing words and loving actions that ease the physical pain and soothe the troubled soul.

How truly awesome it is to watch as the invisible spirit of God takes on visibility through the love and caring of caregivers.

I give thanks to God for caring individuals—instruments through which the inner presence of God is expressed as love. Through their tender touch, caregivers care about and for others.

> "How can we thank God enough for you
> in return for all the joy that we feel before
> our God because of you?"
> —1 Thessalonians 3:9

Inner Treasure

— ◆ —

*My joy is the inner treasure
of Spirit within me.*

What a master teacher Jesus has been down through the ages and continues to be today. His parables are vibrant with spiritual principles. As I apply them to everyday living, I know the joy of living a spiritually enriched life.

My experience with knowing God is a joy that pervades everything I do. I no longer search outside myself for happiness and fulfillment. My joy is the treasure of Spirit that lives within me and is expressed by me.

The joy of the Lord is my spiritual heritage. I open my mind and heart to it so that it can flow through me and out into all of my relationships, experiences, and activities.

"The kingdom of heaven is like treasure hidden
in a field, which someone found and hid; then in his joy
he goes and sells all that he has and buys that field."
—Matthew 13:44

Supported by God

——◆——

*God supports and guides me
throughout my healing.*

If I am receiving some kind of medical treatment in order to overcome a serious challenge to my health, I may at times feel uncertain or even fearful—especially if I do not see immediate positive results. Yet I know in my heart that God is guiding me throughout my treatment time. I envision myself being held by the hand and led to and throughout the right treatment for me.

The best thing I can do now or any time is to pray. Before and during treatment, I give thanks for the healing life of God that is moving throughout my body. I appreciate the variety of treatments that are available and know that there is a method that is exactly right for me.

Whether I am at home or spending time in a medical facility, I give thanks for the wisdom and life of God that are bringing about my healing.

> "Heal me, O Lord, and I shall be healed;
> save me, and I shall be saved."
> —Jeremiah 17:14

Finding Comfort

—◆—

God comforts me with a constant assurance
that surges from my soul.

Being in the familiar surroundings of my home or
neighborhood or in the company of family and friends
comforts and enlivens me. Yet there may be times when
I am in strange surroundings and without the warmth
and companionship of these special people. What do I
do to find the comfort and assurance I need?

Comfort at these times is more than a need to feel
physically and emotionally at ease. I need to realize a
level of comfort that surges from my soul. Knowing
who I am—a spiritual being of God's creation—and
also knowing that the spirit of God infuses me with life,
I am comforted.

God is the source of my comfort. As I live in an
awareness of God and feel the healing presence of my
Creator, my soul is renewed and restored.

> **"As a mother comforts her child,**
> **so I will comfort you."**
> **—Isaiah 66:13**

Strong in Faith

——◆——

I turn all concern
over to God.

What may have seemed so important to me in the past may not be of any or much significance to me now. This is the kind of revelation that helps me understand what is truly important for my growth. Without my realizing it, God has been at work in my life, constantly healing and restoring me. I know that letting go of concern and allowing God to guide me is essential to my well-being. As I do this, I live fully in the present moment and from the presence of God.

When I turn to God for strength, I do not become stressed about everyday matters. I ask myself, "How much will this matter years from now or even tomorrow?" What does matter is that when I let go and let God, I am growing stronger in faith.

As I turn all concern over to God, I feel an immediate sense of relief. Because God is in charge, the solution to the challenge is becoming a reality.

> "That which is, already has been;
> that which is to be, already is."
> —Ecclesiastes 3:15

Spiritual Identity

—◆—

Being the strong and wise spiritual being
that God created me to be, I know true peace of mind.

The spirit of God living within me is the one true constant about me. My outer appearance may change and my thoughts and attitudes may be influenced, but my spiritual identity remains pure and unchanged. With this understanding, I know true peace of mind.

In a time of crisis, I may need to remind myself that God and I are united in eternal oneness. Knowing that I am the strong and wise spiritual being that God created me to be fills me to overflowing with peace.

God calms me with peace when I am stressed, provides me with strength when I need support, and showers me with love when I feel alone.

How blessed I am to live in an awareness of who I am as a spiritual being and to live from the peace of God every day of my life. Then all that I say and do reflects the serenity and faith that fill my soul.

> "But truly it is the spirit in a mortal,
> the breath of the Almighty, that makes
> for understanding."
> —Job 32:8

Positive Attitude

——◆——

*My positive attitude encourages the healing
and renewal of my body.*

The familiar adage of the glass that some see as half
empty and others see as half full is a subtle reminder
that my attitude plays an important role in how I
perceive life and my own health.

If ever I am experiencing a health challenge, I help
with my own healing by having an attitude that is
established on the fullness of life. So I keep my mind
filled with positive thoughts of healing and recovery. I
immediately replace any negative thoughts that may
pop up with positive, healing ones.

Blessing my body with prayers for healing, I give an
energy boost to my immune system. The life of God is
actively at work in my body, and I feel that energy
flowing through me, strengthening and fortifying me
now and for the days ahead.

I am alive with the life of God, and I have a positive
attitude that is constantly supporting this truth!

> "Go in peace. The mission you are on
> is under the eye of the Lord."
> —Judges 18:6

NEVER TOO LATE
BY DENNIS YOUNG

Not all that long ago, I was in prison. And it was there that I made a discovery that brought about a miraculous change in me: I discovered the presence of God. I was liberated! I was free! And everyone else can be set free as well.

God is the one power that sets us all free—free from locked institutions of bricks and bars and free from addictions that have held us in pain and heartache.

This is the message I want to give to people who are suffering. Freedom is not "out there" somewhere. The freedom we long for is always within us. When we make a conscious connection with the spirit of God within us, we are set free!

The person I was seems more like a character from a fable to me now. I hardly know him. The old me was incarcerated at a federal correctional institution for conspiracy to distribute cocaine and other drugs. I had pled guilty to the charge and been given a 4-year sentence.

Because it was my first offense, my indoctrination to prison was this: "You're here because we feel there's hope for you." I had hoped for probation, but the sentence turned out to be a blessing. I'm sure that if I had received probation and gone back out on the streets, I would have gone back to doing and dealing drugs.

Cocaine was my drug of choice, although I began using marijuana while serving in Vietnam. That was the way I coped with the fear—fear of the unknown, fear that at any second I might be killed.

My drug habit became even worse when I finally got out of Vietnam and returned home. I had a family—a wife and three children—but I never saw them. Each day, my whole life—from the moment I got up until I went to bed—was all about drugs and being around people who loved drugs.

My life had become a nightmare, one in which I never seemed to get any sleep. Before I went to jail, I prayed a simple, sincere prayer: "God, help me!"

I soon found out God's answer: "I will help you, but you will get your help in prison."

From 1968, when I first started using, until I was sent to prison in 1984, my life was insane. That insanity stopped the day I entered prison on March 26, 1984. I have never again used alcohol or drugs. I could have scored drugs in prison but chose not to.

I was on the path to freedom, and right at the beginning of my journey, I found *Daily Word* magazine. I read it every day, and the messages gave me hope. I started changing my life from the inside out.

It was obvious that the guards and the staff noticed the change, because they tested me for drugs often. They could not understand why, day by day, I seemed to grow happier. I was actually taking the rehabilitation program seriously.

I read "The Prayer of Faith" in *Daily Word* and memorized it, saying it every morning:

> God is my help in every need;
> God does my every hunger feed;
> God walks beside me, guides my way
> Through every moment of the day.

My life started changing because I was changing. I was doing the things that would improve me. I began exercising. I visited the prison library and found books by Emmet Fox—food for my soul.

I was invited to go outside the prison to speak to kids about drugs. I did it because I wanted to get out of prison for a few hours. The kids liked my honesty, and I think I helped them. God had greater need for me than I consciously knew. And once I started changing my consciousness—knowing that I am always in the presence of God—I felt free, even in prison.

Another inmate saw me reading *Daily Word* and started sharing inspirational books with me. We requested that a study group be started at the prison, and Reverend Carol Record of Unity Church of Northeast Tarrant

County brought the Unity teachings into the facility. This study group is still a strong outreach program there.

I was in prison for 28 months. After my release, I tried to reconcile with my wife and family, but too many things had happened. Too much had changed.

When I was released, the first thing I did was find a Unity church in Wichita, Kansas. I was in a halfway house, and a friend loaned me a bicycle. Every Sunday, I would peddle to church. Marlin White, the minister, saw the hunger I had and fed me spiritually. I began attending the church on a regular basis and became active. I met my present wife in a Yoga class there.

Then I did something that still has some of my old friends shaking their heads in disbelief: I entered the Unity ministerial program. During ministerial training, a friend would call me every once in a while to see if I was still in school. It's a bit hard for him to believe I'm drug-free and a minister as well. I thank God that I'm not the person my friend once knew. I am a new creation.

I've been to the edge—I've even jumped off the edge—but somehow, it was not the end. Someone told me once that the sin is not so much in falling down as it is in not getting back up again. The truth is simple. Whenever we fall down, God is there to help us get up, letting us know that it's never too late to start over again.

TODAY'S MESSAGE:
Transformation

———— ◆ ————

I am being transformed, day by day,
into a shining example of God's love.

God is the one presence and power in all the universe,
and I witness the presence of God's power at work each
day in me, in other people, in the heavens, and
throughout nature.

God's power is within me—power that enables me
to overcome challenges, to be healed, and to transform
myself and my life.

What I most desire to be is a shining example of
God's love. As I act in loving ways, I help transform
conflict into harmony, doubt into faith, hostility into
peace. With love, all good is possible.

Just as a lump of coal can become a diamond, I, too,
am being transformed. My transformation is bringing
out the wonder of God within me. Day by day, the
light of God's love is shining brighter in me and from
me. I am a shining example of God's love!

"Do not be conformed to this world, but be transformed
by the renewing of your minds, so that you may
discern what is the will of God—what is good
and acceptable and perfect."—Romans 12:2

Healthy Communication

—◆—

I communicate with others
with love and acceptance.

Good communication is essential if a marriage or any other kind of partnership is to be successful. In my relationships, I recognize the importance of listening when others are speaking and taking my turn in voicing my opinions.

These are the guidelines I use whether I am communicating with a loved one or someone I have just met. I can always be a communicator of peace as I express unconditional love and acceptance—even if others' opinions are different from mine. I make a commitment to be nonjudgmental and to honor the diversity of everyone.

I recognize that it is not for me to decide whether other people are right or wrong. Rather, it is my responsibility to seek the high road of communication that promotes a healthy relationship and a healthy frame of mind for me.

> "My words declare the uprightness of my heart,
> and what my lips know they speak sincerely."
> —Job 33:3

World of Wonder

———— ◆ ————

Through my faith in God,
I view a world of wonder.

"I will believe it when I see it!" may be a popular expression, yet I know from my own personal experiences that I have been able to perceive some extraordinary things only because I first had the faith to believe.

My faith is in God—not in appearances. So rather than becoming caught up in facts and symptoms, I focus instead on the spiritual connection I have with God. God shows me what is true for me.

No matter how little or how much faith I have, it is enough—enough to enable me to perceive the miracle of life within me and all around me.

I live in a world of wonder—a gift from God that I share with every person and every creature on Earth. Through my faith in God, I can see the magnificent world that is my home and the home of all God's family.

"For we walk by faith, not by sight.
Yes, we do have confidence."
—2 Corinthians 5:7–8

Visualize Healing

———◆———

*As I pray, I envision myself bathed in God's
healing light, and I am healed.*

After I have prayed to be healed of some negative
condition of mind or body, I may or may not notice
immediate results. Yet I know that prayer by prayer, I
am applying layers of healing to both my body and
soul. I keep on believing, and I keep on praying.

My prayer may be an affirmation such as this one:
*God's healing light and love flow through me now. I am being
healed—mind and body.* This is the truth about me:
Divine life does flow through me at all times.

Through my life-affirming prayers, I send messages
of healing to every cell in my body. The response to
the healing power of God is renewed life. As I envision
my body bathed in the healing light of God, I am
visualizing the healing that is taking place, and I am
healed.

> "It will be a healing for your flesh
> and a refreshment for your body."
> —Proverbs 3:8

Whole

— ◆ —

I am whole and complete!

It's true: I may often express a desire to change something about myself—the way I look or the way I act.

Making changes in my lifestyle in order to improve my health or the quality of my life can benefit me greatly, but I remember not to overlook one very important fact: I am a wonderful and complete person just as I am. I am worthy of all the good that God has prepared for me.

It is great to be alive, and it is a blessing to be able to recognize the worthiness and completeness of myself and everyone around me. My understanding of my own self-worth and my appreciation for others are healing practices that promote health in my body and a satisfaction within my soul.

I am whole and complete.

> "Beloved, I pray that all may go well with you
> and that you may be in good health, just as
> it is well with your soul."
> —3 John 1:2

Stepping Forward

———◆———

I release the past
and step forward in faith.

I may think that I have successfully put an event behind me only to find that when memories resurface, so do the hurt and anger. Rather than being healed, I have merely moved my memories of the situation to the back of my mind.

Yet when I truly release any disturbing situation into God's care, I am taking a step in faith toward renewing harmony and establishing peace—for myself and for everyone involved. With God's help, I can leave past events in the past where they will no longer affect me in a negative manner.

I am helping to resolve the situation and also making an investment in a harmonious future. When I meet the people involved, I will be able to greet them with kindness and understanding.

> **"Put away from you all bitterness**
> **and wrath and anger."**
> **—Ephesians 4:31**

I Am More

———◆———

Through grace, I can do
more and be more.

By the grace of God, I am always more than I think I can be. I can always do more than I believe I can do.

Grace is the love of God that goes before me, making my way a path of peace, encouraging me on toward my goals, and assuring me that I am important and needed in God's world.

I am delighted with the results when I trust God to help me through a challenge or to move me forward in an achievement. The joy I experience is a celebration of what God has done through me.

In those times when I seem to fall short of my goal, I realize that, by the grace of God, I can and will do better. The grace of God is there to ease my disappointment and to open the way for something that is even better than what I had been working toward.

"Stephen, full of grace and power, did great wonders
and signs among the people."
—Acts 6:8

Answered Prayer

——◆——

God answers every prayer.

No prayer goes unanswered. Yet the answer to my prayer may not be one that I would have or could have perceived as a reality. I am thankful that the wisdom of God far exceeds my limited understanding.

A whisper within my soul is the gentle assurance that God has heard my prayer. As I pray and speak words of faith, I feel an awareness of God rising from deep within my soul. Then I know such relief! I am at ease—in mind and body.

I am thankful and I hold on to that experience of thanksgiving. God is continually showering me with blessings, reminders that I am loved and cared for by my Creator. My every need is met because God is actively moving in and through me and my life. Whatever my prayer may be, God will answer it, for God is the answer to every prayer.

> "All these were constantly devoting themselves
> to prayer . . . including Mary the mother of Jesus,
> as well as his brothers."
> —Acts 1:14

Meditation

—◆—

"Keep on doing the things that you have learned and received and heard and seen in me, and the God of peace will be with you."
—Philippians 4:9

When the everyday pressures of my responsibilities cause me to feel anxious, I remember that there is a reservoir of peace within me. If I am feeling concern because of family pressures or a work assignment, I turn to God in the quiet of prayer.

I take a deep breath and slowly let it out. As I do, I let the door to my soul open, releasing worry from my mind and tension from my body. Here, in this quiet place, the peace of God gently moves throughout my mind and body. There is mighty power in peace, and I experience it fully.

Then I am ready to go about doing what I need to do. The spirit of God moves from me as a peaceful voice and a loving touch toward my family. I have a new sense of confidence that leads me in being able to tackle any project with the best I have to give.

Prayer

"If God is for us, who is against us?"
—Romans 8:31

God, I have to smile when I think of how confused I must seem at times—especially when I continue to ask for what I think I need while ignoring something greater that You are offering me.

I am learning that my happiness does not depend on material things or accomplishments. My joy in living is knowing You are here with me now and always. Because I know the joy of Your presence, I experience the joy of being with loved ones, for You are the love and life that connects us for all eternity.

You were there, as a presence of vitality that would not allow me to give up on life, when I faced my greatest challenge. You were there with me and my loved ones when a misunderstanding threatened our relationship. I know that it was Your spirit within us that encouraged us to forgive and move on—together.

God, You have always been and will always be with me and my loved ones, and I am so grateful.

DAILY WORD FOR HEALING

Listen, Beloved

—◆—

Beloved,

When the shadows of night have descended and you settle down to sleep, the events of the day may replay in your mind. Thinking about those times, do you understand that I am your constant companion? Simply call on Me, and I will answer.

Now you know that you can always turn to Me for the peace you seek. With this awareness, you experience true peace. Your times of rest refresh you.

Anytime in the future that you need to experience the comfort and assurance of My presence, remember that I am there with you. I will never leave you. There may be times when challenges bring you to your knees. Then pray, hold on to your faith, and draw strength from Me. Remember, beloved, that you are never alone, and I will always love and support you.

"I have said this to you,
so that in me you may have peace."
—John 16:33

Never Alone

— ◆ —

God is my constant companion.

The spirit of God is my companion, lovingly assuring me that wherever I am, I am always on sacred ground and always enfolded in God's healing light.

God is my security and the life that enlivens me. At no time in my life have I ever been completely alone, nor will there ever be a time—now or in the future—when God is not with me.

Because God is my companion, I am able to face each day with a positive outlook and a heart that is filled with peace. God's active, loving presence in my life is the firm foundation on which my serenity and peace of mind are built.

God is a constant presence in the lives of my loved ones as well. What a sense of security I feel in knowing that my loved ones will never be outside God's loving presence!

"Remove the sandals from your feet, for the place on which you are standing is holy ground."
—Exodus 3:5

Oasis of Peace

———◆———

*The peace of God strengthens
and calms me.*

Even in a time of stress, I can spend one quiet moment
in awareness of the peace of God within and be
restored. In my mind, body, and soul, I am refreshed as
I draw from an inner oasis of peace.

The peace of God satisfies a thirst of mind and body
so that I think clearly and act wisely. The clamor of
anxiety gives way to a calm that allows me to hear my
highest and best thoughts. These thoughts are divine
ideas that are the answers to my questions and the
resolutions to all challenges.

In a quiet moment of reflection, inner peace rises up
from within me. I feel at peace and ready to live from
that peace. With a peaceful state of mind and soul, I am
free from tension. In these sacred moments of
awareness, I am infused with strength.

The peace of God is a part of all that I am and all that
I do—and I have the serenity and strength to go on.

"Be at peace."
—Job 22:21

———— 152 ————

Nutrition

———◆———

*God provides me with the wisdom and supply
that enable me to eat healthy, balanced meals.*

Good nutrition is the cornerstone to health and fitness.
And God provides me with all that I need to eat well
and wisely.

Out of the abundance of planet Earth fruit trees
bloom and provide nourishment for my body and a
beauty that stirs the soul. I am grateful for the delicious
and healthy foods I reap from God's bounty.

Deep within Earth's rich soil, seeds take root and
grow upward toward the sun. They spring forth in a
veritable banquet of foods that are laden with the
vitamins and minerals that will satisfy my body's needs.

As I give thanks for and accept the bounty that God
has provided, my mind and body are nourished. I eat
the foods and portions that satisfy me and that contain
all my body needs to stay healthy and whole.

> **"And my God will fully satisfy every need
> of yours according to his riches
> in glory in Christ Jesus."**
> **—Philippians 4:19**

Ready for the Day

— ◆ —

*My times in prayer with God prepare me
for all the blessings of life.*

I want to be prepared for whatever may come my way
in life, but how can I be ready for the unexpected?

Spending time daily in prayer prepares me for the
day. My prayers usher me into a sacred time of being
totally aware of God. In the presence of God, I am
relieved of concerns.

As I listen in the silence, God speaks to me. The
wisdom of God comes to me with such clarity that it
surpasses the knowledge I need in order to make
decisions about my day and my life. My time with God
lays a foundation of lasting faith and trust that assures
me I am capable of handling any situation or challenge.

I am ready for this day and prepared to accept the
blessings that God has for me. My healthy outlook on
life is a positive influence on the way I think, feel, and
act. I am prepared for the expected and the unexpected.

"Prepare your work outside,
get everything ready for you in the field;
and after that build your house."
—Proverbs 24:27

Patience

—◆—

Prayer is the key that unlocks a storehouse
of patience within me.

Being patient with myself is a personal investment that ensures my own success. Being patient with others is an inspiration that encourages them to succeed.

From where do I draw such patience? There is a storehouse of patience and understanding within me, and the key that unlocks the door to it is prayer.

As I pray, I am immediately being fortified with understanding. I know that God is my help in every situation; therefore, I don't have to rely on people or circumstances. By being willing to let things unfold at the right time and under the most enriching conditions, I am applying divine wisdom to everyday life.

Prayer is the key that gains me access to unlimited patience and understanding, which allows me to express the spirit of God in wondrous ways.

> "But as for that in the good soil, these are
> the ones who, when they hear the word, hold it fast
> in an honest and good heart, and bear fruit
> with patient endurance."
> —Luke 8:15

Open to Healing

——◆——

*I am open to God's
healing touch.*

I know that a healing can come in an instant or over time. So I am open to God's healing touch however it comes and whenever it comes.

I have a responsibility to cherish this life God has given me and to live it. I accept this responsibility and consider it to be a blessing. Because of this, I am enthusiastic about helping myself to heal and to stay healthy. My faith-filled attitude is important to my total well-being.

God is the source of all healing, and I acknowledge this no matter where or from whom my help in healing comes. God is the wisdom guiding the doctors during my treatment and also the wisdom guiding me as I make decisions about my own health.

I thank God for creating me for life and for healing me throughout my life.

> "You have made known to me the ways
> of life; you will make me full of gladness
> with your presence."
> —Acts 2:28

Respond with Love

—◆—

*I pray for my loved ones and
for harmonious relationships with them.*

There have been times when the people I love the most
were the ones whose words and actions ignited the
quickest negative reaction in me. This was probably
because of the tension I felt when the people I thought I
knew so well acted in a totally unexpected way.

Since then I have learned not to react but to respond
and to always do so in a positive way. And after just a
brief moment in prayer, I respond with understanding.
That moment of prayer is an investment of harmony in
my relationships.

The same holds true when I am concerned for my
loved ones. While I cannot always be there to care for
them, I know that God is with them always. Each
prayer for them blesses them and helps me to
remember that God is caring for them. I then can release
anxiety about them and remain positive.

> **"And the king will answer them, 'Truly I tell you,
> just as you did it to . . . these who are members
> of my family, you did it to me.'"
> —Matthew 25:40**

Lifetime Commitment

—— ◆ ——

*My lifetime commitment to God
is a commitment to being my best.*

God has blessed me with life, and I am always aware of the importance of this gift and my appreciation of it. I remain committed to taking care of myself by first making a lifetime commitment to God. All I have done or will do is in the presence of God, so I know that God will guide me in being my best.

In my commitment to being my best, I keep my mind alert through my quiet talks with God. During prayer and meditation, God encourages me to be willing to learn all that I can about myself and my world. Because I am willing, I do learn and enhance my experiences in life and my appreciation of my blessings.

I also eat balanced, nutritious meals that are daily building blocks for maintaining and enhancing my well-being. I set aside time for exercise that keeps my body strong and fit. My lifetime commitment to God is a commitment to being my best.

"You shall love the Lord your God with all your heart,
and with all your soul, and with all your mind."
—Matthew 22:37

Meditation

—◆—

"By these things people live,
and in all these is the life of my spirit.
Oh, restore me to health and make me live!"
—Isaiah 38:16

My focus is on the spirit of God within me during quiet times of reflection. Infusing my mind with thoughts that are uplifting and inspired, I realize how full of God's spirit I am.

In silence with God, I consider the whole and holy being that I am: I am filled with ever-renewing life. I am whole in mind, body, and spirit. I am alive and well spiritually, mentally, physically, and emotionally.

The spirit of God within me maintains a harmonious balance that brings me complete well-being and lasting peace as I go about my activities.

Everything I do affects my body, so I am prayerfully thoughtful in my choices. I make the right choices because I follow the divine inspiration I have received. The spirit of God directs my life and keeps me on the right track.

Prayer

—◆—

"Trust in the Lord with all your heart,
and do not rely on your own insight."
—*Proverbs 3:5*

God, there are times when I become so caught up
in solving a problem on my own that I forget You
are always with me and ready to offer a solution to
whatever is concerning me. So I tell myself, "Let go
and let God. Let go and let God."

Each time I come to You in prayer, I am
enfolded in Your love and peace. In this sacred
atmosphere, I release all worries and concerns.
Lingering in Your presence, I receive the purest,
most positive thoughts. I let go and let You
guide me.

Then I feel a release from tension that comes
from being totally in Your presence. My mind and
body are blessed. I feel as if the very cells of my
body are sparkling with renewed energy. In a few
moments of being totally with You, I am
transformed.

I am at peace.

Listen, Beloved

—◆—

Beloved,

You have come to a crossroad in life and have taken the road that leads you in discovering the depths of your spirituality. You understand that every moment can be a sacred time in which you listen with your heart and soul as I speak to you.

So right now, become still and listen. Listen to My message of life and hope. Then allow yourself to feel My presence as a sacred union with you.

You are My child, My creation. Because I love and care for you, I will always be with you—in times of need and throughout all eternity.

Listen, beloved, for I will speak to you within the silence and within the sounds in the world around you. Listen and hear Me in the power surging down a waterfall, as a song that lifts your spirits, as the gentle whisper of wind that blows through the trees, for I am there with you.

"I will help you."
—Isaiah 41:13

God Satisfies Me

—◆—

God, thank You for satisfying
my every need.

Even when my life seems to be in order, I may feel an unexplainable sadness or longing for something more. To discover what it is I desire, I tap into that feeling and trace it back to its source. Yes, within my soul is where it began—as a desire for a greater awareness of God.

One of my basic human needs for health of mind and body is to know that I am a spiritual being. I know I am because the spirit of God resides within me. The more aware I am of God, the more I am aware of and accept the healing life of God that is being poured out to me.

The more I know of God, the more I let the life of God live out through me. Whenever I long for more, I know it is the fullness of my realization of God that will satisfy me.

"Bless the Lord, O my soul . . . who satisfies you with
good as long as you live."
—Psalms 103:1,5

God-Break

— ◆ —

Resting in silence
with God renews me.

When I need a boost of physical energy during the day, I eat a wholesome snack to reenergize myself. When I need a boost of spiritual energy, I rest in silence with God during a prayer break.

Giving my full attention to God stimulates me. In this quiet time of communion, I awaken my whole being to life and healing.

Resting in silence uplifts me mentally and emotionally. The clatter of my thoughts gives way to a sacred hush. Feelings of peace refresh me in an instant. Breathing deeply and fully, I feel a completeness of spirit, mind, and body.

I emerge from my time of rest renewed in mind and body. Willing to take on the day but, if needed, to move at a leisurely pace, I am enthusiastic about life. I am revitalized by my time of rest with God.

"Return, O my soul, to your rest,
for the Lord has dealt bountifully with you."
—Psalms 116:7

Acceptance

———◆———

*Thank You, God, for loving me
and accepting me just as I am.*

During my growing-up years, I may have felt that
belonging to a certain group or club would cause my
peers to accept me. Looking back, I now realize that
how other people perceive me is not nearly as
important as how I perceive myself.

I am a unique individual with my own skills and
abilities. As a child of God, I try always to bring
special light and love to each experience. Through what
I think and say and do, I make a positive difference in
the world.

Even when the people closest to me do not
understand or accept me the way I am, I know that God
does. God sees into the very depths of my being and
knows the love that fills my heart.

Yes, God does love and accept me, and I love and
accept others as I work with God to bring the healing
balm of acceptance into my world.

"I will give thanks to you, O Lord. . . .
For your steadfast love is higher than the heavens."
—Psalms 108:3–4

Preparing to Receive

——◆——

*God, in asking, I am preparing
to be blessed.*

I know that when I let go of a problem, what I am giving up is worry and stress. I also know that because of this release, I will be aware of and cooperating with the perfect solution that God is bringing about.

Yet if ever I seem to struggle with letting go and letting God, I think about Jesus' spirit-filled directions: "For everyone who asks receives, and everyone who searches finds, and for everyone who knocks, the door will be opened" (Luke 11:10).

I am asking, and I know that I will receive my good. I am searching, and I know that I will discover the right path to take. I am knocking, and I know that the very door to abundant life will open to me.

All this and even more is possible because all things are possible with God.

"I love those who love me,
and those who seek me diligently find me."
—Proverbs 8:17

Focus

—◆—

*Focusing on God guides me
in making the best decisions.*

In the midst of a healing crisis, I may be tempted to make a decision that is based on fear or confusion. Even though I know that I should be focusing on my healing, I may find it difficult. So I take that necessary step back to see the bigger picture with all things in their proper perspective.

I can make this shift when I give my full attention to God. The spirit of God within me is the wisdom I need to make the best decisions concerning my health and well-being.

My emotions will not limit me when I focus on the presence of God—in me and in others. So I can be confident that my choices about my health care will be the very best ones for me.

"I have now come out to give you wisdom
and understanding. At the beginning
of your supplications a word went out, and I have come
to declare it, for you are greatly beloved. So consider
the word and understand the vision."
—Daniel 9:22–23

Serendipity

——◆——

Today is filled with divine serendipity—
blessings awaiting my discovery.

Like gold nuggets shining brightly in a shallow
mountain stream, there are blessings just waiting to be
discovered by me. Like the passerby who goes to that
fresh, clear stream for a sip of water and also discovers
gold, I appreciate that God blesses me with more than I
need or expect.

God is so good to me, blessing me with life and
vitality—treasures worth more than I could imagine.
Appreciating life is an experience of divine serendipity:
I discover that God is blessing me with something more
valuable than anything I could envision or desire or
pursue.

So I know that even in the midst of what may seem
like a disappointment or challenge, there is renewal for
me—all by divine serendipity!

"I will make them and the region around my hill
a blessing; and I will send down the showers
in their season; they shall be showers of blessing."
—Ezekiel 34:26

New Beginnings

—◆—

*New beginnings infuse me
with hope and enthusiasm.*

Even before the blossom of a vibrant and glorious flower begins to fade and wither, the circle of life is continuing: Seeds of new life are being formed. What would seem to be an ending has become a new beginning.

My life, too, is a process of seeming endings that become new beginnings, a process of growth and learning, of healing and starting over.

As I learn more about God and my own spiritual nature each day, I am infused with new hope and enthusiasm for life.

As I share the joy and expectation I feel for life with others, I do so freely—without expectation of anything in return.

The life of God is continually nurturing me. I know there are bright new beginnings ahead for me and my loved ones.

> "The grass withers, the flower fades;
> but the word of our God will stand forever."
> —Isaiah 40:8

My Hope

———◆———

God is my hope.

The future may seem like a great mystery, for it is so full of possibilities and unknowns. There is no limit to what I could experience or what might happen during the next year, the next day, or even the next moment.

The physical reality is that I can live only in the present moment. The divine reality is that I always live in the presence of God. So when I hear dire predictions about the future, I take a reality check. I see a future of hope because I know that God is with me now and will always be with me, guiding me as I explore the wonders that are awaiting my discovery.

Knowing God in every moment of life and feeling my connection with God at all times prepare me for a fulfilling life—now and in each new moment of the future. God is and always will be my eternal hope, joy, peace, and love.

"For surely I know the plans I have for you,
says the Lord, plans for your welfare and not for harm,
to give you a future with hope."
—Jeremiah 29:11

Our True Identity
By Mary L. Kupferle

hen the person who had been the most loving, supportive individual in my life died, I had to rebuild my own life.

Bill and I had been married for 57 years, spending the major part of our lives together as a couple. Although I had my own work as a Unity minister, I had been Bill's wife for much longer; we were partners in life.

With Bill gone, I had to begin to understand again who I was. After some soul-searching, I realized that my true identity is not as anyone's relative—no matter how great and wonderful that relationship may be. My true identity is as a child of God, and my relationship with God affects every other relationship I have or could have in life.

Although I know this is the truth about me, this spiritual identity has not always been easy for me to hold on to—especially now that the one person who had been so much of everything I had ever done is no longer with me.

What I also realize is that this beloved person, my husband, was a child of God, just as I am a child of God. And we are eternally one through a divine kinship. Perhaps for the first time, I really understand that my husband and I were each intended for certain experiences in life, experiences that developed our own individual identities as children of God.

And no matter what those experiences may be for any of us—from life to death to everything in between—we are never alone. God, our creator, is always right there with us at the very core of our being. Because we know this, every experience can bring us a greater awareness of God and a greater awareness of the importance that every individual must give to his or her soul development and growth. Although we may feel lonely at times, we are never alone.

This awareness has sustained me through everything that has happened—even Bill's passing. I understand that he was, is, and always will be a part of God. And because I am a part of God, Bill and I are forever one.

When we listen to and believe in the One who tells us, "I am with you always" (Matthew 28:20), we will be blessed by the understanding of our oneness with our Creator. We will be blessed in grief and in sadness and in whatever we are experiencing.

Within just a few days of Bill's passing, I had to dig deeper into an understanding of my oneness with God. One afternoon, I fell in my home and broke my leg. I could not move, so during the next 4 hours, I lay on the kitchen floor and waited for someone to discover my plight and help me.

Lying there on the floor, I focused on all the things I had ever learned in Unity about praising God, giving thanks, and knowing that God is with me. I sang songs and I prayed.

I filled those 4 hours with faith in God. Occasionally I would call out for help; the door from the kitchen to my backyard was open, but I wondered if anyone could possibly hear me.

In a moment of what I can only describe as divine timing, my neighbor stepped into her backyard just as I was calling out. She and her husband ran to my house, found me, and called 911.

The people who helped me in the hospital, in rehabilitation, and in my home since then are those whom I call illumined people. They are so open to God.

As they sat by my bedside and talked with me about God, our differences in religion or culture did not matter. Some were Protestants, some were Catholics; one was from Ethiopia, and another was from China. Yet each one of us knew we were one family of God. We believed together, and I thank God that we did, for such belief speeded up my healing.

Years ago I learned about the power of prayer from a feature in *Weekly Unity* magazine called "Someone Prayed." As I read, I began to understand that God loves me—all the way through my being. I learned that I can bless and praise my body and know that the spirit of God within every cell will respond with renewing, healing life. This is true for everyone, and we can support each other in knowing this and living this belief through prayer.

That article caused me to reach out to the positiveness of the Unity principles and to follow the teachings of Jesus. I could have traveled many paths that are interesting and perhaps more elaborate, but the simplicity of the path I chose still affects me: God is good.

As a child of God, I am an expression of God's good in my world. This is my true identity and purpose in life, and this is the good news that is true for us all.

Sacred Stirring

———— ◆ ————

The sacred stirring within my soul
is a response to God's presence.

Whenever I feel confused or frightened, God reassures
me. I feel God's spirit stir within my soul, relieving my
mind of worries. A sacred presence surrounds me and
fills me with a renewed sense of security.

With that sacred stirring, my soul awakens to God
and longs to know more of the holy Presence. I feel an
infusion of energy and receive an abundance of creative
thoughts.

With God's presence to guide me, I am renewed in
purpose. My purpose is to live in divine light and be a
channel through which divine life and love flow.

Mere words cannot begin to express my gratitude for
the joy I feel. Each day is one in which I continue in a
closer communion with God, and each day I feel
renewed as the sacred stirring within my soul responds
to God's presence.

"Call to me and I will answer you."
—Jeremiah 33:3

God in Me

— ◆ —

God in me is life, light,
and love.

The spirit of God within me is the spirit of life and love that sustains me in every moment of my life. I am aware of a divine kinship that unites me and every creation on Earth, for the spirit of God, who created all, is within all.

God in me is life—healing life that nourishes and renews me.

God in me is light—a guiding light of wisdom and understanding that gives me the insight I need to make wise decisions about my health and well-being.

God in me is love—love that is unconditional and everlasting.

Yes, the spirit of God is within me always. Every move I make, every step I take, every word I speak, and every breath I take is infused with the spirit of God.

> "Do you not know that your body
> is a temple of the Holy Spirit within you,
> which you have from God?"
> —1 Corinthians 6:19

Strength and Energy

———◆———

*The power of God within me is my source
of unlimited strength and energy!*

Beginning each day with a few minutes of prayer and
meditation, I build a spiritual strength that keeps me
uplifted throughout the day—every day. Spiritual
strength enhances my enthusiasm for life and a
commitment to strengthening myself physically.

The spirit of God within me is my source of
unlimited strength. In quiet times of making a conscious
connection with the power of God within me, I
experience interludes of rest and relaxation. In times of
busy activity, I discover a reserve of energy that I can
draw upon.

Even when I am constantly on the go because of a
full schedule at work or at home, I remember to take a
prayer break. I am relieved of stress and allow my
reserve of energy to be replenished.

I have a strength and energy born of Spirit—God's
presence within me.

> "I will strengthen you, I will help you."
> —Isaiah 41:10

Foundation

——◆——

*My relationship with God is the foundation
on which I build my life.*

A house is only as strong as the foundation on which it is built, so only the strongest materials and structurally sound plans are used in the construction of this important base.

I also build a strong foundation for my life—a spiritual foundation that supports me with the strength to make it through any challenge. My relationship with God is the foundation I create, one prayer at a time.

Prayer keeps me in touch with the spirit of God within—the spirit of life and love that nurtures and sustains me. This sacred relationship is the firm foundation for my relationships with others.

My faith in God assures me that I will always receive the love and support I need. I am blessed with wisdom and strength.

> "Blessed are you, Simon son of Jonah! . . .
> I tell you, you are Peter, and on this rock
> I will build my church."
> —Matthew 16:17–18

Healthy Bones

———◆———

*I bless the intricate network of bones
in my body with prayer.*

I try never to take anything about my body for granted,
and I certainly want to ensure that my bones are strong
and supportive.

Including foods that contain calcium in my daily
meals and exercising properly help maintain and rebuild
my bones, so I make it a point to eat right and to follow
a routine of exercise that fits my needs and my lifestyle.

Posture is important too. I remember to sit and stand
tall, so that my back and shoulders are in a comfortable
and natural position. There is much I can do to help
keep my bones strong and healthy, and what a pleasure
it is to make an investment in my own health.

One of the best investments I can make, however, is
prayer. This spiritual approach to healthy living is one
that blesses every bone in the intricate network
throughout my body.

> "You are in the Spirit, since the
> Spirit of God dwells in you."
> —Romans 8:9

Refreshing My Memory

—◆—

My prayers and my positive attitude
refresh my memory.

It is no wonder that when I walk from one room into another, I may occasionally forget what I am going after. My brain is very busy: Besides controlling my thinking, it adjusts my heartbeat, blood pressure, and other functions. With billions of nerve cells, my brain constantly processes incoming information and outgoing commands.

Temporary forgetfulness can be frustrating; however, I understand how impaired memory can cause people to become moody and affect their personalities, decision-making ability, and even the way they move and walk. My heart and prayers go out to those who are experiencing such life-changing challenges and to those who are their caregivers.

I also pray for my own memory. I stay mentally and physically active so that my thinking and memory are at their best. What an important difference my prayers and positive attitude make in refreshing my memory.

"Be renewed in the spirit of your minds."
—Ephesians 4:23

Creation of Life

— ◆ —

*I am one of God's
marvelous creations of life.*

I may have been praying for a healing in a specific area of my body; however, today I feel a strong urging to bless my whole body. I know with greater clarity what a work of divine design my body is.

Each cell, organ, muscle, and bone contributes to my total well-being. There is a cooperation between mind and body that promotes healing. So I have a deep commitment to ensure that everything I think and do is in agreement with my total health and absolute wholeness.

I am learning more and appreciating more about my body. The fluid movements and functions that my body performs are incredible feats that no amount of technology could produce. I am God's child, living and expressing my spiritual nature in a body of marvelous design. I will remember that all children of God are wonderful creations of life.

> "It is that very Spirit bearing witness
> with our spirit that we are children of God."
> —Romans 8:16

Restful Sleep

— ◆ —

*In total awareness of God, I experience rest
and refreshing sleep.*

How good it feels to lie down and let the bed support
my body while my muscles relax. I am ready for a good
night's sleep. Then, if I let myself, I can start thinking
about the problems and events of the day and become
anxious!

A sure way back to peace of mind is to think about
God. I may even think of myself as cradled in the palm
of God's hand. I am safe. I have no worries. There is no
past or future; there is only now, only me, only God.

I breathe deeply as I release all awareness of my
physical surroundings. I am serene as I close the door to
the day and open the door of my soul to God. My
body is relaxed and my mind is calm.

I am aware of God and God is aware of me. What
better place, what better space could I be in for complete
rest than in the presence of God? I drift off to deep,
restful sleep, knowing I am fully supported by God.

**"When you lie down, your sleep will be sweet."
—Proverbs 3:24**

Meditation

—◆—

"I appeal to you . . . that all of you be
in agreement and . . . that you be united in
the same mind and the same purpose."
—1 Corinthians 1:10

I embrace my loved ones in spirit through a quiet time of prayer and meditation.

Knowing that God's love unites us heart to heart and soul to soul, I close my eyes and quietly speak the names of those I am praying for today.

God knows the people that I am concerned about, yet speaking their names brings me a greater awareness of my unity with them.

One by one, I visualize each person and see that person healthy, strong, and enjoying all that life has to offer. I envision my loved ones glowing with the life of God.

I bless my loved ones as I include each one in this heartfelt prayer:

"God, thank You for the blessings these people bring to my life. May they always know Your love in all that they do and in all that they are."

Prayer

—◆—

*"But overhearing what they said, Jesus said
to the leader of the synagogue,
'Do not fear, only believe.'"*
—Mark 5:36

God, when I am away from my loved ones, my
heart aches and I feel alone. Then something
remarkable happens when I pray: I feel hope rising
within me. I know the peace of being totally
connected with You and with them.

I have faith in You, God. Therefore, I know
how it feels to be free from worry and stress. Your
peace is my comfort and strength, and Your
wisdom is my constant guide. Softly and tenderly,
Your love infuses me with renewed hope and
inspiration.

God, I hear You calling me, and I listen to all
that You have to share with me. When I am weary,
You lift me to heights that I never before dreamed
were possible. Whenever I start to have doubt, I
remember that You are with me and my loved
ones and I am secure.

In all that I do, I know that You are caring for
us as a loving parent would, and I am at peace.

Listen, Beloved

—◆—

Beloved,

Allow the truth of My words to abide within your soul:

You and all those you hold dear are My creations of life and love. I created you to live healthy and happy lives.

You are ageless and eternal—magnificent creations of life and joy. The spark of My own creativity continues to flow within each of you, ensuring your connection with Me and a unity of spirit with one another.

I am in you and you are in Me. My spirit is the foundation of who and what you are, and it is My spirit within you that inspires you to accomplish whatever you set out to accomplish.

When a relationship or a way of life comes to an end, trust in Me and let go of any doubt that you may have about starting over. It is never too late for you to begin again, for you and your loved ones are ageless and eternal masterpieces.

"I will make you majestic forever,
a joy from age to age."
—Isaiah 60:15

Being of Life

—◆—

*I am an eternal being
of life!*

Whatever my age is now or at any time in the future, I won't allow any label such as "too young" or "too old," "too qualified" or "underqualified" to limit me.

There is so much of life for me to live, and I want to experience it in all its glory. So I work on having a positive attitude. Then I am aware of the good that is happening to me and through me.

Even as an adult, my body is still changing. Maybe the changes are not as apparent as they were when I was a growing child. Still they are taking place, and I recognize them as an ongoing process of life.

I am blessed in knowing that I am an eternally evolving being, a creation of God still in progress. One of my heartfelt desires is to be the very best I can be at every age. I will need help, and what a relief I feel in knowing that God is my constant help.

"Surely goodness and mercy shall follow me
all the days of my life."
—Psalms 23:6

I Am Comforted

———◆———

In the sacred activity of prayer,
God comforts me.

More than likely, there will be times when I feel as if I am starting over in life. Whatever the situation, it is only natural that I find comfort in what is familiar to me. A favorite song or a familiar face soothes my mind and emotions.

When it comes to finding lasting comfort, I turn to God—the constant Presence that I know will always soothe my soul.

Turning to God in prayer opens the window of my soul and invites divine serenity to come in. Then, any uncertainty about my health and well-being is dispelled as I linger in the presence of God.

In times of change, I know that God is my greatest source of comfort. In the sacred activity of prayer, I am comforted.

> "I call upon you, O Lord; come quickly to me;
> give ear to my voice when I call to you."
> —Psalms 141:1

Courage

— ◆ —

*I am courageous; my courage is built
on my faith in God.*

Am I going through something that requires an extra
measure of courage? Maybe I am waiting on the results
of a medical test or need the courage to break free from
a negative habit.

I can be brave when I know that courage flows from
my faith in God. God is expressing life through me
now, and I have a strength of mind and body that aids
in my own healing and recovery. I expect the best and
know that no matter what may appear to be happening,
God is healing me.

I may not realize how strong my faith is until a
challenge appears. The courage I have may at first
amaze me. Then I feel so right about being courageous
because I am stepping out in faith—faith in the Creator.

God within me is always capable of great and
wonderful things.

> "Wait for the Lord; be strong, and let your heart
> take courage; wait for the Lord!"
> —Psalms 27:14

Breath of Life

——◆——

The breath of life is a gift from God that sustains and supports healing within me.

With each breath I take, I fill my lungs with life-sustaining oxygen. Filled with the breath of life, I continue to live and grow and function.

Every breath is a gift from God, for every breath sustains and supports the healing activity within me. Every breath is one that renews and restores me to health and wholeness.

The life of God permeates the very atmosphere around me and blesses every expression of life. In a miraculous cooperation, I share the breath of life with plants and animals and humans alike.

As I breathe in slowly and fully, I give thanks for the breath of life. I give thanks for a gift that nourishes and upholds me in every moment of life.

> "By the word of the Lord the heavens
> were made, and all their host by
> the breath of his mouth."
> —Psalms 33:6

Inner Mystery

———◆———

*God reveals what is true: I am free
in mind, body, and spirit.*

At times, it almost feels as if some inner mystery is surfacing in my mind, seeking to be revealed. I may sense that some discontent is stirring or some idea about a change is taking root, but I cannot quite identify what it is.

As I spend time in prayer, however, I discover that God is guiding me to free my mind of worry, to contemplate new opportunities. What seemed like a mystery is transformed into a revelation of how the spirit of God within me is my freedom to do and be my very best.

With all my being I am free. There is no habit or dependency that can limit me. God within me is freedom of mind, body, and spirit—freedom to let go of what is no longer good for me and freedom to accept a healthier lifestyle.

I live life fully and freely because I am aware of the presence of God. The inner mystery that is revealed by God is my freedom and life.

"You were called to freedom."—Galatians 5:13

Welcome Home!

——◆——

Turning to the spirit of God within,
I experience a true homecoming.

I feel instant relief from the tension I have felt when traveling on a dark and stormy night as soon as I see a light shining from a window of my home. That light welcomes me home.

I receive that same feeling of "welcome home" in my relationship with God. No matter how gloomy outer circumstances may appear, the light of God's spirit is always shining within me, dispelling the darkness of doubt and revealing my way. In the sanctuary of my soul, God welcomes me home.

The spirit of God shines brightly within me, energizing me and giving me a new zest for living. I am able to remain focused on what I need to be focused on, and I feel at peace about the new life that is unfolding before me. Embraced by the love of God, I experience a true homecoming.

> "I love you, O Lord, my strength.
> The Lord is my rock, my fortress,
> and my deliverer."
> —Psalms 18:1–2

TODAY'S MESSAGE:
Work in Progress

——◆——

*Each day holds the promise
of new life.*

Looking at people and nature, I understand that all of God's creation is a work in progress. Divine creativity is active everywhere, bringing out life, love, and beauty.

Creativity resonates in the tune that comes from the instrument being played by a child or a master musician. God is not finished creating through the master or the child, for both are works in progress. Their music improves and grows sweeter each time they play.

God is not finished with me either, for I am a work in progress. Each day holds the promise of new life for me, and I can hardly wait to experience the wonder that God will express through me today as health and a joy in living.

> "Your people shall all be righteous. . . .
> They are the shoot that I planted, the work
> of my hands, so that I might be glorified."
> —Isaiah 60:21

God's Light

——◆——

*The light of God shines in and through
my thoughts and my life.*

The warm glow of a candle is a comfort to me,
because it is a reminder of the eternal light of God that
is in everyone and that shines everywhere throughout
the world.

So if I have been struggling to make sense of a
situation or to understand why someone said or did
something that was hurtful to me, I stop struggling. I
remember that the light of God, the presence of the
Creator, is shining in me. Divine light brings me
comfort and peace.

The light of God is always within me, but it is up to
me to let it shine into my thoughts and my life. I do this
when I am open to God's wisdom and guidance.

God will never fail me, for divine light leads me step
by step, moment by moment, through every challenge,
achievement, and opportunity of life.

> "You led them by day with a pillar of cloud,
> and by night with a pillar of fire, to give them light
> on the way in which they should go."
> —Nehemiah 9:12

Meditation

—— ◆ ——

*"Your eye is the lamp of your body.
If your eye is healthy, your whole body
is full of light."*
—Luke 11:34

In a time of meditation, I close my eyes and just allow them to rest.

As I affirm their continued good health, I can literally feel a lessening of muscle tension and eyestrain. I am uplifted in spirit and move beyond the physical and into the spiritual realm.

In this quiet time, God blesses me with an inner, spiritual vision that enables me to more fully recognize the beauty of life and my world.

I give thanks for the precious gift of sight and for the sweet glimpses of the divine I experience in everyday happenings.

Relaxed and at ease, I am able to see so much more than the physical world of color and contrast and texture.

My eyes give me a view of my world, and these blessed instruments of light and vision bring me greater insight into my world.

DAILY WORD FOR HEALING

Prayer

—◆—

"He sent out his word and healed them."
—Psalms 107:20

God, just speaking Your name enlivens me.
Your name resonates within my body and soul,
awakening me to Your presence.

In Your presence, God, I feel alive and
renewed. When I think of You and the reality of
Your spirit within me, I feel aglow with life.

How amazing it is that a thought of You or a
prayer to You can cause me to feel renewed! Yet I
understand that thoughts and words are powerful
healing tools.

God, thank You for giving me life and for
renewing me with life. I realize that there is no
negative condition that can withstand Your
healing, restoring power.

I hold a sacred vision of Your power moving in
and through me. I feel alive and fulfilled because
You are constantly renewing me with life.

DAILY WORD FOR HEALING

Listen, Beloved

—◆—

Beloved,

You are wonderfully made—shaped and formed to be vitally alive. There is life and intelligence within every cell of your being that respond to your thoughts and words. So think thoughts of life, speak words of life, and live life fully.

When you look into a mirror or touch your face, you are beholding the magnificence that you are. You are a vessel of divine life! The perfection of your inner spiritual being shines from you, so recognize it and claim it. Let the light of your spiritual nature shine through your eyes and all that you say and do.

You may not fit the standard of others because you are unique, not standard! Dare to be unique, for from this uniqueness you will contribute greatly to the people around you and to life itself. Daring to believe in yourself, you will also believe in others and encourage them. What you see in yourself and all people is a reflection of Me.

"Thus says the Lord who made you,
who formed you in the womb and will help you:
Do not fear."—Isaiah 44:2

DAILY WORD FOR HEALING

I Have a Choice

———◆———

In the quiet with God,
I am at peace.

Some of the choices I make are so simple I don't even need to consciously think about them. For instance, in the dark of night, the choice I make to turn on a light so that I won't stumble and fall is an automatic one.

Yet, what choice do I have when one stressful situation after another is popping up around me? I can always choose to turn to the peace of God within me so that I won't become stressed.

I give my mind, body, and nerves a rest as I close my eyes and think about the spirit of God at the center of my being. I breathe in deeply. As I breathe out, I release all tension from my body and all worry-thoughts from my mind.

In the quiet, I discover the peace of God that is always there for me to experience and to rely on. I am at peace with God.

> "Then they were glad because they had quiet,
> and he brought them to their desired haven."
> —Psalms 107:30

Wake Up to Renewal

—◆—

*My words of healing are a wake-up call
to renewal for my whole body.*

I speak powerful healing words that are the truth about me: "Through the presence of God within me, I am healed!" Then, remaining quiet and still for a few moments, I allow these words of healing to resonate throughout my body.

Words of healing and even thoughts of healing carry a message of God's presence throughout my body. They are a call to life and health and well-being for me.

I speak words of healing to my heart, my lungs, my bones, my whole body: "Through God's presence within me, I am healed!" I live my life believing I can be healed and expecting goodness.

I praise God for the healing that is constantly taking place.

> "He welcomed them, and spoke to them
> about the kingdom of God, and healed
> those who needed to be cured."
> —Luke 9:11

Song of Joy

— ♦ —

I sing a song of joy
and praise to God.

As I listen I can hear it—a song of joy that is resounding throughout my body. The same sound of joy that rises from the delicate sparrow and the mighty waterfall rises from within me as well.

My own heart joins in the chorus of thanksgiving because I am filled with the joy of Spirit. There is joy in being alive and in being an integral part of God's world. Recognizing my own importance in the greater scheme of things magnifies God and God's creativity. I add to the fullness of God's joy by expressing my own joy for life.

God is so good! In heartfelt appreciation for the magnificence of my own life and the creation of all the world, I sing a song of joy and praise to God.

"Let the heavens be glad, and let the earth rejoice;
let the sea roar, and all that fills it;
let the field exult, and everything in it.
Then shall all the trees of the forest sing for joy."
—Psalms 96:11–12

Thankful Heart

—◆—

My heart overflows with thanksgiving.

There is so much in life to be grateful for that I may lose count of all the blessings I experience in just one single day.

Yet when I am paying attention to my body, I am presented with new wonders every day:

Through the intricate working of nerves and lenses, my eyes show me a world of beauty and awe-inspiring creations.

The ability to hear and think and speak and move around with ease are wondrous blessings that also help me live life more completely.

I cannot help but have a thankful heart because my heart is overflowing with my appreciation for God and all the ways that I am blessed.

Each new day is a wondrous time of discovery, a time for giving thanks for all my blessings.

"Let the word of Christ dwell in you richly;
teach and admonish one another in all wisdom;
and with gratitude in your hearts sing psalms,
hymns, and spiritual songs to God."
—Colossians 3:16

Serenity

—◆—

God fills me
with blessed serenity.

Oh, what blessed serenity I experience as I turn to God in prayer. Here, in a sacred communion with God, I receive the peace and assurance I seek.

God heals me and gently restores me. In prayer, I feel divine life moving through me and soothing me. There is an interaction of life between me, the created, and God, the Creator. I know true peace.

As I come away from my prayer time, I bring with me a heightened awareness of God and God's presence in my life. That awareness continues to help me remain peaceful and calm.

My desire is to live each moment fully aware of God. My awareness of God blesses me with a serenity that is beyond description. It is a serenity that says to my whole being, "Be at peace."

> "Peace I leave with you;
> my peace I give to you."
> —John 14:27

Companions and Friends

—◆—

Thank You, God, for creating
animal companions and friends.

Animals communicate with people in a language of the heart. How great it is to be welcomed home by a pet: the dog that is so vigorously wagging his tail that his whole body wiggles, the cat that is so determined to be recognized that she continues to meow until she receives a hello.

Then, as I reach down to my pet, I am uplifted in mind and heart. Petting dogs and cats calms them and also reduces my feelings of stress, which is often reflected in lower blood pressure and peaceful feelings.

Yes, God did a great work in creating animal companions, so I remember to bless my pets and animal friends and to thank God for each one of them.

"So out of the ground the Lord God formed
every animal of the field and every bird of the air,
and brought them to the man to see what he
would call them; and whatever the man called
every living creature, that was its name."
—Genesis 2:19

Enough Faith

— ◆ —

I have faith in God.

If I ever doubt that I have enough faith to meet some challenge or to accomplish a goal, I remember what Jesus taught about faith. He shared the truth that faith—even faith the size of a tiny mustard seed—has the power to move a mountain of challenges out of the way.

I have faith in God. I trust God to show me what to do when obstacles appear in my way and to give me the strength to overcome whatever I need to overcome.

Reinforced with faith, I make great discoveries. I spend less time worrying and more time interacting with the people who are important to me. I am at ease, so I truly enjoy the companionship of family and friends.

Most important of all, my faith inspires me to continually deepen my relationship with God.

> "If you have faith the size of a mustard seed, you will say to this mountain, 'Move from here to there,' and it will move."
> —Matthew 17:20

Thoughts of God

—— ◆ ——

*Every thought of God is a prayer
that comforts me.*

Whenever I am feeling alone or confused, I take a moment to acknowledge that God is with me. My faith reinforces that acknowledgment so that any feeling of insecurity or confusion dissipates.

Every thought of God is a prayer. How amazing it is that I am only a faith-filled thought away from finding release from feelings that are pulling me down. The way up and out of negative emotions and habits is to remind myself that God loves me.

When I begin to talk to God in prayer, I experience the loving presence of my Creator in every fiber of my being: "God, thank You for being with me in this moment and in every moment of my life. In the comfort of Your loving presence, I receive new strength and energy."

> **"For your steadfast love is before my eyes,
> and I walk in faithfulness to you."
> —Psalms 26:3**

YES, GOD IS LISTENING
BY BILL GOSS

D iagnosed with cancer at age 38, I was told I had only a few months to live. But I had everything to live for: a beautiful wife, two great kids, and an exciting career as a Navy pilot.

I had realized my dream of breaking the sound barrier—in an F/A-18 Hornet. The next day, I felt a small bump on the back of my left ear and went to the doctor. He looked at the clear, skin-colored bump and said, "Commander Goss, it's harmless."

Not one to worry, I still felt led to get a second opinion—from the flight surgeon. She reassured me, "Commander Goss, it's a harmless fatty cyst."

I started to walk away and then turned back to say, "Hey, I came here to have this thing removed. Cut it off!"

"Okay, okay, I'll cut if off," she said. We laughed and joked as she sliced my ear open, scraped out the bump, and put a stitch in my ear.

A week later, I was called into the office of an ear-nose-and-throat surgeon. He told me I had malignant amelanotic melanoma, a rare form of cancer without the telltale dark discoloration. Not able to look me in the eye he said, "Listen, you could be dead in 6 months." What I realized he was saying was that I *would* be dead in 6 months!

I was sick with grief at the thought of leaving my wife and children to find their way without me. Early one morning, about a week after the diagnosis, I couldn't sleep and went outside. Standing barefoot in the sweet-smelling grass, I looked up at the star-studded universe and prayed, "God, if You are listening to my prayers, please, oh please, show me a sign." I waited and waited, face pointed to the sky. Nothing!

But just as I started to go inside, the largest meteor I had ever seen streaked across the sky. I started to cry. I felt as if God was lighting my way to a healing. I knew as perhaps I had never known before that God is real, prayer is powerful, and faith, even a small amount, means everything. I had a renewed feeling of hope after seeing God's monster meteor. I began to learn everything about malignant melanoma that I could.

Studying at the library, searching the Internet, talking to doctors, I learned that melanoma is aggressive. Early detection and aggressive treatment armed with a supercharged immune system are important to healing. A supercharged human spirit is the key to supercharging the immune system.

I knew intuitively that the only way to supercharge the human spirit is to have faith—faith in God, faith that

DAILY WORD FOR HEALING

things will get better, faith in your family and friends, faith in your ability to have fun, and faith in your ability to focus on the problem.

I underwent 12 hours of surgery. My left ear was cut off down to the earlobe. My jugular vein as well as my trapezius muscle and salivary system were removed. I looked like a Frankenstein monster. The doctors told me my face would be paralyzed and I would never be able to smile again. (My face has zero paralysis, and I smile a lot.) They said I would have very restricted shoulder movement. (I do 80 fingertip pushups every morning.) They refused to do plastic surgery on me until I had survived a year.

A year later, I was at the plastic surgeon's door. After 10 operations, my ear was rebuilt—from a piece of my rib and skin from my groin. Today, even on close inspection, no one could tell that anything had been wrong with my ear.

During that year of waiting, I exercised and kept my thoughts positive. I kept building a strong faith and a strong immune system. Hearing the diagnosis of cancer is almost synonymous with hearing, "You are alone." You feel alone and destroyed of hope. And when hope is destroyed, the immune system implodes. It collapses on itself. So I never lost faith in God; I had hope!

I have been cancer-free for more than 5 years. As an inspirational speaker, I share my story of resilience and

DAILY WORD FOR HEALING

hope on television and radio shows throughout the world. Now producers want to turn my book into a movie.

If I were told I was going to die tomorrow, I would have no fear. I would have profound sadness that I was leaving my wife and kids to fend for themselves. Yet I believe God is like the ocean and my life is like an eyedropper full of that ocean. When my life as I know it ends, the eyedropper that is me will go back into the ocean. Then I will instantly explode into all the wonderfulness of God.

Faith in Action

———◆———

I am faith in action!

I may not be called upon to tackle a mountain of a problem every day. If the occasion should arise, however, I know that my faith, combined with my creativity, allows me to move that challenge or to move me around and past it.

I am stepping out in faith by being a doer rather than an observer. God gives me unlimited resources of strength, wisdom, and love. I use these qualities to the fullest extent of my understanding of them. I am faith in action!

I want every word I say and every action I take to flow from my faith in God within me and my faith in God all around me. My prayer is one of thanksgiving:

"Thank You, God, for showing me that my faith is a stepping-stone to a more fulfilling and productive life."

> "Faith by itself, if it has no works, is dead. . . .
> Show me your faith apart from your works, and I by my works will show you my faith."
> —James 2:17–18

Creation of God

———◆———

*As God's creation, I have been created
to express life!*

I live in a world of God's creation—a world that
provides all I need to live and grow and thrive. Yet there
may be things that happen to me and around me that
do not seem to be orderly or fit in to my image of a
world of order.

Because I can never know all there is to know about
everything, there are some things in life for which I have
no reasonable explanation. But my faith in God assures
me that even when things happen that I do not
understand, there is still divine order underlying every
event in my life.

Just as God created the heavens and the earth, God
created me to express life.

I am God's creation of life!

> "For thus says the Lord . . . who formed
> the earth and made it (he established it; he did
> not create it a chaos . . .): 'I am the Lord,
> and there is no other.'"
> —Isaiah 45:18

Clothed in Glory

——— ◆ ———

I am clothed in the glory of God.

What about me is self-repairing, heat-resistant, water-resistant, and so pliable that it conforms to my shape? My skin, which does all this and even more. It also helps to keep my body temperature stable through pores that breathe and perspire.

I am clothed in the glory of God and sustained by the life of God. I can observe the miracle of life taking place with the healing of a scratch on my arm. Soon after the scratch takes place, there is only the hint—a tiny line—that any trauma took place.

And when a more serious condition occurs, I know and affirm that my skin has the same ability to heal from that condition as it did from a scratch. Of course, I do all that I know to do to cooperate with the healing activity. I protect my skin from too much exposure to the sun, and I maintain a healthy eating plan. This is the least I can do to show my appreciation for such a wonderful gift.

> "Moses did not know that the skin on his face shone
> because he had been talking with God."
> —Exodus 34:29

Words of Light

— ◆ —

*My kind and loving words to others gladden
their hearts and gladden my heart, too.*

The kind words spoken to me by loved ones or friends instantly brighten my day. I can brighten their day, too, with cheerful, loving words.

Helping to uplift others is something that blesses me too. I feel good when I see a happy response on another person's face. It's a pleasure to shine the light of love and appreciation on someone else.

I know also that anytime I allow my comments to and about others to be less than loving, I can hurt them and myself. So I don't let my words create feelings of negativity and regret in me. How enjoyable my relationships are when I am kind and when I encourage kindness from others!

I am blessed by every word that goes forth from me to gladden the hearts of others.

> "If you are wise, you are wise for yourself;
> if you scoff, you alone will bear it."
> —Proverbs 9:12

Abundant Life

—— ◆ ——

*God is the source
of abundant life.*

Although there are many different people and
experiences that bless me, God is the source of abundant
life. Whenever I am feeling a lack of energy or anything
else, I remind myself to look to God for my blessings.

I know in my heart that my good will come, but
when bills are demanding to be paid immediately, I
may begin to feel doubt. However, I won't let that
doubt linger to cloud my view and keep me from
accepting a blessing that is just waiting to be claimed.

Giving thanks to God focuses me on my true source
of abundance. Then I recognize the blessings that I may
not have noticed previously. I do not hesitate to claim
new blessings as they present themselves. I am alive
with the abundant life of God, and I am blessed beyond
measure.

> "Every work that he undertook in the service
> of the house of God . . . he did with all his heart;
> and he prospered."
> —2 Chronicles 31:21

Words of Life

—◆—

*I speak words
of life!*

Words are so much a part of life. My words are actually expressions of my life. If I am having a difficult time expressing myself, I pray about it.

Speaking my prayers aloud to God, I make each one a composition of words of life. I hear how I sound when I am in the presence of God; I am confident and at ease.

When I speak to a group, I help myself gain confidence and be at ease when I remember that God's presence is with me. I am not alone in speaking to any number of people; I am supported by God.

Words of life can also help me if I have a difficulty with speech or I am learning a new language. When I have patience with myself as I speak, I do my very best in speaking. If I sense that people do not understand me, I may repeat a sentence or even rephrase it. Words of life work wonders through me.

> **"My lips will shout for joy
> when I sing praises to you."
> —Psalms 71:23**

Set the Pace

———◆———

*I set a pace for a lifetime
of accomplishments.*

Every runner begins the race with a desire to win.
Runners in a long, arduous race know to set a pace
so they have the energy to run the full distance and
even win.

I, too, set a pace in my life for goals and
accomplishments, for some of the most worthwhile
ones come about over a period of time. I intend to
make progress throughout a lifetime, so I won't accept
something simply because it offers some sense of
immediate gratification.

Because I have set a pace, I am not constantly rushing
around. Taking time to rest refreshes me and keeps my
goals in clear focus. I enjoy life while I am living it,
taking time to be with family and friends and taking time
to relax. Savoring the experience of life, I truly appreciate
every day for the tremendous gift from God that it is.

"Put these things into practice, devote yourself to them,
so that all may see your progress. Pay close attention to
yourself and to your teaching."
—1 Timothy 4:15–16

Source of Joy

———◆———

God created me to express joy—
today and always.

Finding a moment of joy in the midst of a health challenge may be difficult, but it is possible when I remember that God is always with me.

In every instant of my life, God is my true source of joy. I am God's creation of joy, and expressing joy is just one way I let the "real" me shine forth.

The real me is a spiritual being, a creation of light and life that radiates the joy of Spirit. As I allow my inner light to shine, I am learning that joy is a gladness of Spirit that is not just for some days, it is for all days.

Even in the midst of a challenge, God's joy is waiting to pour forth from within me and to be a part of every experience in my life.

God fills my life with joy-filled moments. This day is just one of many that make up a lifetime of joy.

> "Let all who take refuge in you rejoice;
> let them ever sing for joy."
> —Psalms 5:11

Meditation

—◆—

"Come to me, all you that are weary and are carrying heavy burdens, and I will give you rest."
—Matthew 11:28

If I am having difficulty releasing the worries of the day and am finding it almost impossible to relax, I need to gently encourage myself to let the relaxation I need to experience become a reality.

I begin by finding a quiet place and closing my eyes so that I will not be distracted. As I shut out the world from my physical view, I gently release any concerns I may have into God's care.

If thoughts of the day try to intrude, I do not struggle to keep them away. Rather, I recognize them and then let them go, knowing that I will get back to them later at a more appropriate time.

Gradually, my mind becomes quiet. Then, as I envision it happening, my body begins to relax. From my toes up to the top of my head, I experience a time of rest and renewal.

A feeling of serenity flows throughout my body. I am blessed by my time of doing nothing but allowing myself to be in the presence of my Creator.

DAILY WORD FOR HEALING

Prayer

— ◆ —

*"Listen, children, to a father's instruction,
and be attentive, that you may gain insight."*
—*Proverbs 4:1*

God, thank You for always being there when I turn
to You for love and comfort. I listen, God, as You
speak tender words that soothe my heart and heal
my soul. You hold nothing back as You give me the
understanding I need to overcome any challenge
and also the inspiration to follow through even
when I doubt that I can.

Your presence is everywhere, God. What
reassurance I feel when I know that it is Your spirit
shining out through the gentle smiles of loved ones
and strangers alike. Divine ideas sparkle like gems
in conversations with friends, coworkers, and
acquaintances.

How blessed I am to know You, God, and
how grateful I am each time I become quiet and
listen to You. Yes, God, I am listening, and I feel
Your healing presence surrounding me now.

DAILY WORD FOR HEALING

Listen, Beloved

—◆—

Beloved,

There will be times when change comes about in your life. As each change occurs, you can and will find the courage and strength to make the right choices, for I will be with you each time and for all time.

You will no longer define *change* as something that causes doubt in your mind. You will feel a sense of excitement because you realize the potential and opportunity that will come about as a result of a change.

Because you include Me in your decisions, you will feel at peace with all that the future may hold. Life will offer many doors of opportunities for you to pass through. If one door closes, turn and face the next opportunity with confidence, for I have opened another door for you. Step forward in faith, dear one, and eagerly accept what awaits you.

"The Lord is good, a stronghold
in a day of trouble; he protects those
who take refuge in him."
—*Nahum 1:7*

A Work of Love

——◆——

I am a work of love
created by God.

I enjoy a healthy, happy life as I remain aware of the presence of God. There may be times, though, when I feel as if I am losing ground—moving two steps back for each step forward. Appearances may suggest that I am not making any progress, but when I see myself as a work still in progress and still learning, I realize that every experience of my life has a purpose. While I may not be able to see the big picture right now, each step is bringing me closer to a clearer understanding and to my goal.

My life is a work of love created by God. So rather than labeling a mistake "a failure," I look at my life with a spiritual vision that alerts me when God is encouraging me to move in a new direction. I am confident that with each step I take, I am making progress, for I am gaining a greater understanding of myself as a work of God's love.

"Do not neglect the gift that is in you."
—1 Timothy 4:14

Unlimited Love

—◆—

God's love for me
is unlimited and constant.

A change of seasons can be a vivid, physical reminder of how transient life is. As lush greens turn to orange and red and as warm breezes become laced with a hint of winter's chill, something deep within me responds to the changes taking place around me.

Yet no matter how many of these physical changes take place in my body or in my life, one thing will always remain unchangeable: God's unconditional love for me. God loves me with a love that knows no limits—a love that transcends time and place and circumstance, a love that heals and soothes my soul in extraordinary ways.

I am grateful that I understand change is a natural part of life. Rather than reacting to change with worry or fear, I give thanks for something that never changes: God's unconditional love for me.

> "Do not be afraid, little flock, for it is
> your Father's good pleasure
> to give you the kingdom."
> —Luke 12:32

Immune System

———◆———

*God created me
to be well.*

The ability of my immune system to ensure my health is miraculous. My body has been created by God with all the capabilities to overcome disease—from serious illness to the common cold. I have been created not only to survive but also to flourish.

So if I have a cold or am facing a challenge of a more serious nature, I bless my body in prayer and then let God guide me in what to eat and what actions to take that will allow my immune system to work at optimal capacity.

Perhaps I am guided to get some rest. Or maybe I will be led to seek the advice of a medical professional. Whatever God leads me to do, I do with a joyful heart, because I know that I am on the way to complete recovery. My immune system is truly amazing, and I give thanks for my body's ability to heal itself—through the life of God within me.

**"I am going to bring it recovery and healing."
—Jeremiah 33:6**

Active

———◆———

I am active in mind,
body, and spirit.

Whether I am able to exercise at low or high levels of activity, I am doing something to relieve my mind of stress and to condition my body. I might start out slowly, building up to a routine that involves cardiovascular benefits. Getting started and sticking with it are two choices I make, choices about which I need divine support. Still, I know God is willing and ready to help me.

An active mind and an active physical routine are part of a healthy, fulfilling life. Yet the most important ingredient to health of mind and body is to be active spiritually. Prayer and meditation, thanksgiving and praise have a positive, healing effect on me. I know this is true because I feel so alive when I am fully in the presence of God through prayer and meditation.

The activity of my mind, body, and spirit blesses me with renewed vitality and health.

"You see that faith was active along with his works,
and faith was brought to completion by the works."
—James 2:22

Learning More

———◆———

The spirit of God helps me to learn more
and to remember more.

Technology is advancing rapidly on a daily basis—at home and at work, in school and in just about every area of life. I am constantly encountering new ways of doing things—ways that make my tasks simpler yet also require that I learn more than ever before.

In such a fast-paced world, I may wonder how I can possibly remember all that I need to recall. Yet I can and do remember, because the spirit of God within rejuvenates my memory.

Memory is a valuable tool that I use in storing a vast amount of information so that what I need is available to me when I need it. I have peace of mind while going through any kind of test, and such peace of mind helps me achieve the results I desire to achieve.

"Get wisdom; get insight: do not forget,
nor turn away from the words of my mouth."
—Proverbs 4:5

Pray for Others

——◆——

I honor God and bless my loved ones
in the sacred activity of prayer.

What an honor it is when someone makes this request:
"Pray for me." And how loved and appreciated I feel
when someone says, "I am praying for you."

I hold others in high esteem as I pray for them, but
most important, I honor God as I pray:

"God, I am praying for my loved ones, knowing that
Your spirit is within them, guiding and healing them
now and always. I experience such peace about them in
the realization that Your spirit within us and within the
very air separating us is a powerful connection that can
never be broken.

"In my own times of challenge, I can feel—beyond a
shadow of a doubt—that others are praying for me. I
receive this blessed assurance as it radiates from the
depths of my soul.

"Prayer is a sacred activity that honors You and
honors Your presence of life and healing in us all."

"Beloved, pray for us."
—1 Thessalonians 5:25

My Senses

—◆—

*God blesses me with the ability to fully experience
the sacred presence in all and through all creation.*

Through my senses, I am keenly aware of my world
and the people in it. So I bless my senses in prayer:

"God, bless my eyes. They serve as my window to
the world. With my eyes and my faith in Your
greatness, I will never cease to be amazed at the beauty
that surrounds me.

"God, bless my ears. Through Your miracle-working
power, I am blessed with an intricate yet delicate
system of cartilage and nerve endings that allows me to
hear. The sounds of the life You have created echo
around me and fill my soul with the sound of joy.

"God, bless me so that I am aware of You as I touch,
smell, and taste the wonder of Your diverse creativity.
As I go about my day, I use these senses countless
times, and I always pray that they bring me a greater
awareness of Your presence in all and through all
creation."

"In him we live and move
and have our being."
—Acts 17:28

Beacon of Light

— ◆ —

*I am a beacon of God's light
in my world.*

In a storm-tossed sea, a lighthouse stands as a beacon of light for those who are lost and searching for land.

I, too, am a beacon of light when I let God's spirit shine forth from me to encourage and support others. In the midst of chaos, I shine the healing light of God on the situation so that a divine plan can be revealed. People know that I will accept them just as they are, so they feel comfortable expressing their true thoughts and feelings to me.

My kind words offer comfort to those who feel as if they have been tossed about by the storms of life. I care about them and show how much I care by quietly listening to them. Sometimes, when they speak their deepest thoughts aloud to me, they hear for the first time what they can do to let their own inner light shine more brightly.

"Let your light shine before others, so that
they may see your good works and give glory
to your Father in heaven."
—Matthew 5:16

Meditation

—◆—

"Peace be within you."
—Psalms 122:8

I take a few moments to create a peaceful
atmosphere within my own mind. I do this by
turning my attention away from my busy day and
even the most seemingly urgent matters.

Closing my eyes, I invite positive, God-
centered thoughts into my consciousness. I am
patient with myself when a troubling thought
comes to mind. I gently release that thought as I
silently affirm: *The peace of God is within me, and I
make a vital connection with divine peace now.* Peace, the
sweet peace of God, answers my need for serenity.

Resting for a few moments in this awareness, I
realize true peace of mind. I can and do bring that
peace back to my day and all my activities, and I
share it with others.

What a difference being peaceful makes in all
that I do. I have peace of mind and I help others to
know that peace of mind is their reality also.

Prayer

— ◆ —

*"A glad heart makes
a cheerful countenance."*
—Proverbs 15:13

God, my joy is in knowing that Your spirit of life
and love and joy is within me at all times. My heart
is filled with the peace of Your presence.

It is with a glad heart that I go about this day.
What I feel in my heart, I also convey in my
conversations with others. I want my words to
sparkle with life and vitality so that they shine light
on the time I spend with my family and friends.

God, there may be times when I am feeling
less than joyful about a situation, but as I let Your
spirit be a part of my thoughts and actions, I am
preparing myself to expect and accept a blessing. I
know, God, that You are always blessing me.

Yes, I have a peaceful heart that is reflected in
everything I do, because I know that Your spirit is
within me.

Listen, Beloved

—◆—

Beloved,

Let go of worry, let go of fear, and let Me ease your mind.

Allow My love to fill you. Feel the peace that comes from knowing that you are always in My care and keeping.

Trust in Me, beloved, and know that you are not alone. I am always with you to help you and support you.

Let go of any concerns you may have for the days and weeks ahead. Let Me guide you to happiness and wholeness now.

My love for you knows no end. As you let go and let Me work in and through you, you will begin to see more and more of My love in every area of your life.

My life is your life. Trust in My life within you to bring about your healing.

"Commit your way to the Lord;
trust in him, and he will act."
—*Psalms 37:5*

DAILY WORD FOR HEALING

Step by Step

——◆——

The light of God is divine wisdom
that guides me and inspires me.

When I listen in a sacred time of prayer, God speaks to me, alleviating my worries and concerns. So I listen with an open mind and heart, and God shines the light of understanding on me and on every situation in my life.

What love I feel in the light of God's presence! How uplifted I am in spirit! Every doubt is being washed away in the cleansing tide of God's love. I am ready and willing to follow divine guidance.

Step by step, God shows me what to do to mend any past hurts or regrets. I give thanks for the wisdom that is guiding my feet and for the love that upholds me. There can be no doubt that I am held in the tender embrace of my Creator.

Always I turn to the light—the wisdom of God that is my guidance and inspiration.

"O send out your light and your truth;
let them lead me;
let them bring me to your holy hill."
—Psalms 43:3

Rejuvenated

——◆——

The life of God within me is healing me.
I am rejuvenated.

As I rub my hands together briskly, I feel the warmth that is generated as energy is released. This physical activity reminds me of a spiritual activity that is taking place within me at all times: the activity of Spirit that is continually healing and restoring me.

The spirit of God fills me with energy, and I am rejuvenated. As I concentrate on the life of God within, I feel the response of life at the very core of my being. New energy flows throughout my body and revitalizes me.

I am one with God and one with the life of God that is present throughout all creation. Through my eternal spiritual connection with God, I am sustained by a renewal of life. God is always aware of me, for I am tenderly held in the hollow of God's hand.

> "In his hand is the life of every living thing
> and the breath of every human being."
> —Job 12:10

God Is More

———◆———

The spirit of God within me
is bringing out qualities through me.

Am I happy with myself, or do I feel I could use a bit of improvement? Well, it is important that I remember there is more to me than what I may appear to be. There is always more, for the spirit of God lives in me.

The spirit of God makes me more—more loving, kind, intelligent, and whole—more of what I want to be and all that I am capable of being.

Should appearances ever tempt me to judge others, I remember that the spirit of God lives in every person as something more, which I may not be able to see. Then I will not react to appearances but will, instead, look for ways to appreciate people.

I thank God for being more in them and me and for giving more through us all.

> "Look at the birds of the air; they neither sow
> nor reap nor gather into barns, and yet
> your heavenly Father feeds them. Are you not
> of more value than they?"
> —Matthew 6:26

Up Moments

—◆—

I recharge my spiritual battery
by opening myself to God's holy presence.

If ever I am feeling down, I bring myself up by
recharging my spiritual battery. I do this with prayers of
healing for my mind and body:

"Dear God, I open my mind to Your holy presence.
Realizing that my thoughts directly impact my day and
my health, I keep them focused on You. What a
blessing this realization brings me.

"Dear God, I open my heart to You and experience
immediate relief from painful memories. You love me
unconditionally, and Your love soothes me and
encourages me to love.

"Dear God, I open my life to You. I will never need to
face anything alone, for You are with me. You satisfy
every longing of my soul and refresh me with a new
enthusiasm for life."

"O God, you are my God, I seek you,
my soul thirsts for you."
—Psalms 63:1

My Digestive System

———◆———

*God encourages me to relax
and eat healthy.*

Eating in a rush is never a good idea; however, there are times when, because of a tight schedule, I feel pressured into eating a hurried meal. The impact of that hurry may not be apparent as I am eating, but afterward, the discomfort I feel will make me aware that my digestive system is stressed.

So if I find I have a tendency to rush, I remember how important it is to slow down, relax my mind and body, and enjoy my food. This commonsense approach blesses me for hours after I have taken my last bite.

With some cooperation from me, the digestive system that God has designed will work smoothly and efficiently. I am calm, and that sense of well-being is reflected in my eating habits. God encourages me to relax, and relaxation helps keep me healthy and strong.

"To this end we always pray for you, asking
that our God . . . will fulfill by his power
every good resolve and work of faith."
—2 Thessalonians 1:11

God Is In Charge

—◆—

God is in charge.

In spite of what is happening around me or to me, I affirm that all is in divine order and that order will prevail because God is in charge.

God is the master creator of everything and everyone—every person and animal, every star and planet in the universe. And God is in charge of all.

When events in my life seem to be taking me in a direction that I do not want to go or I am feeling as if I am not as healthy or peace-filled as I would like to be, I remember God's promise: "Know that I am with you and will keep you wherever you go" (Genesis 28:15).

God is with me now and forever. I may not understand why I am experiencing a particular challenge; however, I do know that God has a greater plan that brings order to my life. Through every moment of my life, God is in charge. The assurance of God's presence and care brings me peace of mind.

> "Know that I am with you and
> will keep you wherever you go."
> —Genesis 28:15

Stress Relief

———◆———

*God's spirit within me is my constant source
of peace and serenity.*

To escape the stress of the day, I allow my thoughts to
take me within to the presence of God.

I relax in this atmosphere of pure, unconditional love
where no anxious thoughts can remain. In the presence
of God, I am one with a serenity that fills me and
soothes me. The peace I first experienced in my
thoughts moves throughout my entire being. I relax so
that my heart rate is strong and steady.

The peace I feel is more than a temporary occurrence.
It is a tangible awareness that will remain with me
throughout the day, for God's spirit—the source of my
peace—is within me always.

The experience of prayer refreshes and renews me.
As I return to the activities of the day, I remain peace-
filled and serene, for God's spirit is within me.

"They refreshed my spirit as well as yours."
—1 Corinthians 16:18

Healing Faith

———◆———

*God is actively
healing me now.*

In the midst of a large crowd, one woman showed tremendous faith. She knew in her heart that she needed only to touch the clothes Jesus wore and she would be healed. She did and was healed immediately.

I, too, can be healed, for I, too, have tremendous faith—faith in God and in the power of God within me. God's healing life is a stream that flows continuously throughout my body—renewing cells and bringing new life to those areas that need to be healed.

Yet divine life is so much more. It is the spiritual connection I share with God and with every other person on Earth—a connection that links us in mind and heart as we pray for health and wholeness. United in prayer and faith, we can overcome any challenge to our health.

> "Your faith has made you well; go in peace,
> and be healed of your disease."
> —Mark 5:34

LISTENING WITH THE HEART
BY KATHY NELSON

W hen my telephone rang on an October morning in 1989, I wasn't expecting to hear news that would so drastically impact the lives of my family: "Mom, there's been an accident—with the girls. . . . " My daughter Lori's voice trailed off, and then there was silence.

"Are Jennifer and Julie all right?" With all my heart, I wanted to believe that my granddaughters were okay.

With a catch in her voice, Lori continued: "Jennifer has a broken pelvis, but the doctor says she is going to live. But, Mom, the outlook is different for Julie."

Lori started crying but went on: "It looks like Julie's not going to make it. Her head is so totally crushed that the doctors at the trauma center don't even know what to do for her. Oh, Mom, they told me they've never had a patient with such a severe head injury."

Jennifer and Julie had gone for a ride in the back of a pickup truck with a 16-year-old friend who was driving them through the hills around their California neighborhood. Reaching a speed of 60 mph, he lost control, and the truck smashed head-on into a palm tree.

Thirteen-year-old Jennifer was thrown clear of the truck. Julie, who was 11 years old, was thrown forward with such force that she left a dent the size of her head in the back of the cab. She flat-lined—showed no detectable vital signs—three times, once on the way to the hospital and twice in the hospital.

I thought I was prepared for what I would see by the time my husband, David, and I arrived at the hospital, but I wasn't. Julie's face was as big around as a dinner plate and totally flat. She had no facial features—except eyes that were so swollen that they stayed closed for about 3 weeks.

Because Julie was in such a fragile condition, the doctors could not give her a full examination. They advised, "We will try to keep her stabilized, and then just wait and see." We waited, praying that she would live.

On the 3rd day, David and I, along with several of our friends from church, were in the hospital waiting room. David, who is a quiet, private person, asked if the rest of us would join hands with him in prayer. As the circle of friends held hands, David prayed a beautiful prayer of surrender: "God, we are holding a vision of Julie whole, healthy, and complete—either with You or with us. We release her to You, God, because You know best."

At that moment, I felt a surge of energy; it seemed to pass from one of my hands, through my body, and out the other hand. I felt sure everyone in that circle had felt something. My friend Phyllis hugged me and said, "Kathy, Julie is going to be okay." I responded, "Yes, I know!"

On the 11th day, Julie showed no signs of improving.

Still Lori held a vigil at her daughter's bedside. A nurse, working for the first time in the pediatric ICU, was checking on Julie when she turned to Lori and asked, "Does your daughter know sign language?"

"Not that I know of," she answered.

The nurse continued checking Julie's breathing tube and IV connections. "Yes," she said, "I'm sure she's trying to signal us. I saw her finger move!" She positioned a pen in Julie's hand and slid a tablet under it.

Slowly the 11-year-old began writing a message to her mother: "I'm in here! How's Jenny?"

Julie improved each day after that. She began to breathe on her own and responded when people came into her room. Two weeks after the injury, she was able to undergo reconstructive surgery. Six doctors worked 13½ hours putting Julie's face back together. They referred to photographs of her as they worked, and once the swelling went down, the result was a beautiful girl.

When one of the doctors came out to talk to us after surgery, Lori gave him a big hug and said, "Thank you for saving my little girl." He held up his hands and said, "I was only the instrument. God does the healing."

The staff called Julie their miracle girl. They had never seen anyone come back so whole from such a severe head injury. Several articles were written by her surgeons because her surgery and recovery were groundbreaking.

Still, they expected that Julie's recovery would take at

least 2 years. In 3 months, she was back in school. Her eyesight was perfect. She was an A student before the accident and a B student after she returned to school— and the only reason she went from an A to a B was because she had missed so many school assignments.

We wondered if Julie was aware of anything from the time of the accident until she came out of the coma, and this is what our little 11-year-old told us:

"I remember being in the ambulance, and a man with red hair and a green shirt was working over me.

"In the hospital, I could hear people talking, could see people in the emergency room. I felt as if I were looking down at me. I saw my face, and couldn't believe it looked so bad. I couldn't understand why everybody was so upset, because I knew I was going to be okay. I kept wanting everybody to know I was.

"Then the whole room was bright and shiny and I heard a voice. But I heard it with my heart, not with my ears. It said, 'Do you want to go or do you want to stay?'

"I thought about it and answered, 'I really like where I am, and I need to go back to help my mom. Besides, who would take care of my cat?' "

Julie listened with her heart, and has taught a lot of people how to do this. She is 21 now, attending college, and working in a day care center with children. Julie is still listening with her heart, and she's well on her way to making a significant difference in the world.

Miracle of Life

———◆———

Created by God, I am
a miracle of life!

What do I see when I am looking at a picture of me? Do I see a ready smile and a love for life shining from my eyes? That is a wonderful picture, but I am so much more than what I or others may see with the eyes! I am a miracle of the wondrous power of God!

All people are miracles created by God, and I, too, reflect the joy and love of my Creator. Being animated with life—able to move, think, and act—is the greatest miracle of all.

The confidence I feel is based on the understanding that I am capable of achieving so much more than I can ever imagine is possible. How encouraging it is to know that I can always be more and do more. I celebrate the miracle of life by eagerly participating in the beautiful mystery of life that God is unfolding through me.

"Peter answered him, 'Lord, if it is you, command me to come to you on the water.' He said, 'Come.'"
—Matthew 14:28–29

Spiritual Connection

— ◆ —

*As a caregiver, I make a heart-and-soul
connection with people.*

When people reach out to other people with love and
compassion, a powerful spiritual connection is made.
The spirit of God in the caregivers flows out to uplift
the spirits of people in need of comfort and care. There
is also a response from the spirit of God within the ones
being cared for.

Giving and receiving care creates a heart-and-soul
connection that blesses those who give and those who
receive. Just watching the look of concern or fear melt
away and a smile spread across the face of the person
being cared for, I actually see the powerful effects of
love in action.

What an honor it is to care for God's creations!
Caregivers bring out the best in themselves as they give
from compassionate, loving hearts, and they help to
bring out the best in the ones who receive the care.

> "He sustained him in a desert land, in a howling
> wilderness waste; he shielded him, cared for him,
> guarded him as the apple of his eye."
> —Deuteronomy 32:10

New Opportunities

—◆—

*The spirit of God is helping me
with every new opportunity.*

A healing can come in various forms, including endings, beginnings, and new opportunities. But an ending that is not of my choosing—to a relationship, a job, or a way of life—can be a shock. Even though I acknowledge there is need for a change, I may still have much to work through.

I will help myself and those who are dear to me by knowing that every ending is the introduction to a new beginning and new opportunities. Although I may feel anxious about a change, I do not let such a feeling rob me of the belief that I can do whatever I need to do in my new beginning.

I believe in more than myself; I believe in the spirit of God that is moving in and through me, providing me with the wisdom and strength I need.

> "So then, whenever we have an opportunity,
> let us work for the good of all, and especially
> for those of the family of faith."
> —Galatians 6:10

TODAY'S MESSAGE:
At Peace about Others

———◆———

*God is with my loved ones wherever they are,
wherever they go.*

There may be critical times when I cannot be with
my loved ones or even be in touch with them. Yet
worrying about them during those times does not help
them or me.

My faith encourages me to believe the best for them.
Faith reminds me that God is the life and health, the
wisdom and peace that are always available to my
family and friends.

If there is a time I feel concern about my loved ones, I
strengthen my faith though prayer:

"God, although I am separated from those I love,
they are always on my mind and in my heart. Thank
You for caring for them and for sustaining them with
life. I am able to be at peace about them knowing that
You are constantly guiding them and loving them.
Through Your spirit within us, we are forever united in
love. Thank You, God, for being with us wherever we
are, wherever we go."

"God is with you wherever you go."
—Joshua 1:9

Guide to Activity

———◆———

*God is my guide to activity that blesses me
in improving and maintaining my health.*

I know that I am unique—everyone is. Yet do I remember to consider my own uniqueness as I make and carry out decisions about my health and the way I exercise? Surely it is something worth praying about:

"I need Your guidance, God, so that I know what to do to improve my health and to maintain it. The right kind of exercise and the number of times I exercise are important. I realize my optimum level because You have designed my body to let me know when I overdo. Yet when I have been inactive, it's amazing how both my mind and body awaken when I take a brisk walk.

"It has taken me time to reach the shape I am in today. If I am not satisfied, I can do something positive about it. The sure and steady commitment I apply each day brings me lasting results. This I believe is my guidance from You."

**"You are indeed my rock and my fortress;
for your name's sake lead me and guide me."**
—Psalms 31:3

Eyes

———◆———

I behold the beauty and majesty
of God everywhere.

My eyes take in light and then send impulses to my
brain so that I capture the color, forms, and shapes of
the world around me. I see beauty and also majesty, for
I see the glory of God everywhere.

I appreciate and take care of these precious organs of
sight by protecting them from direct sunlight and
irritating dust. If my vision does need correction, I thank
God for glasses, contact lenses, or medical procedures
that enable me to see clearly.

Most of all, I am thankful for an inner vision that
beholds the presence of God within me and others. In
times of prayer and meditation, my physical eyes may
be closed in an attitude of reverence, but my inner eyes
are alert and seeing.

With my physical eyes I can see people, but with
inner vision I behold God's presence within them. What
beautiful sights I see.

> "The night is as bright as the day,
> for darkness is as light to you."
> —Psalms 139:12

Sacred Retreat

—◆—

A sacred retreat is a time in
which my soul is renewed.

How good I feel when I am able to get away from the whirl of daily activity for a while! Even if it is only a short retreat from my regular routine and responsibilities to be consciously aware of God's presence, I am rejuvenated. I plan the time for the renewal of my soul.

My spiritual retreat is also a time of preparation for whatever happens afterward. Relaxed and at peace, I am prepared for any eventuality and can handle what only a few moments before would have caused me to feel stressful.

Whether I take a few moments at home or on the job, or spend a couple of weeks in some vacation spot, I want my experience to be a sacred time of renewal. From this time of renewal, I experience a resurgence of energy and creativity that I then apply to my current goals and projects or to new ones.

"Jesus took with him Peter and James and John,
and led them up a high mountain apart, by themselves.
And he was transfigured before them."
—Mark 9:2

Language of Love

—◆—

*I express love through an unspoken language
that everyone understands and appreciates.*

People around the world communicate in many
different languages. Newborn babies seem to have their
own language of sounds. Yet even when someone is
speaking in a language unknown to me or when I am
trying to decide the needs of a baby, I understand a
language of expressions, not words.

A smile is the universal sign of welcome by one
person to another. When holding a newborn, I
understand that when the baby is sucking its fist, it
might be saying, "I'm hungry!"

My nonverbal expressions speak to others as well, so
I maintain an attitude of loving-kindness that is reflected
in a smile and a gentle touch. I am relaxed and at ease,
which helps put others at ease in my presence. Most
important, I share the joy of love with others—
whatever languages they speak.

"So they remained for a long time, speaking boldly for
the Lord, who testified to the word of his grace
by granting signs and wonders to be done through them."
—Acts 14:3

Meditation

—◆—

"Get up and go on your way;
your faith has made you well."
—Luke 17:19

When I think healthy, positive, divinely inspired
thoughts, my body responds with the energy of
God-life.

So in the silence of prayer, I bless my body
with reassuring words of appreciation and
encouragement:

I bless my kidneys, for they help keep my
body free of impurities.

I bless my back, giving thanks that it is both
flexible and strong.

I bless my shoulders, arms, and legs for the
fluid movement and agility they provide me with
as I move about.

Glowing health is the ideal condition of my
body and mind. Turning to God in this sacred
moment of prayer and meditation, I establish a
balance so that mind and body work together
toward health. The rejuvenating life of God within
me responds with a healing.

Prayer

—◆—

"Prosper for us the work of our hands—
O prosper the work of our hands!"
—Psalms 90:17

God, bless my hands and guide me in using them
in service to You. Make them strong and supple,
yet tender and sure as they reach out to help those
in need.

My hands are Your hands, God, and they bring
comfort and reassurance to others. With a tender
touch, they soothe doubts and fears and remind
others that we can share Your love with each other.

My feet are Your feet—blessed reminders of
the support and understanding You give to me. As
I walk and run, my feet take me farther and farther
along in my life's journey. Along with my hands,
my feet are blessed instruments through which I
can be an extension of Your love and care.

There is a spark of Your creativity within me,
God. Show me the ways I can help to create an
atmosphere of acceptance and love wherever I am.

Listen, Beloved

—◆—

Beloved,

Have faith in Me, and through that faith you will understand that My grace is eternal and offers you unlimited blessings.

I am continually renewing you with life. To help you understand the blessing of renewal, picture in your mind a plant blossoming in springtime. Now watch, for even before one bloom withers and fades, another bloom appears.

Have faith in Me, beloved, for just as surely as each spring holds the promise of life and renewal for the plant, each moment holds the promise of life and renewal for you. The opportunities for the renewal of your mind and body are as unlimited as My love for you.

As your faith in Me continues to grow, your awareness of My presence will increase. Continually renewed with life, you rejoice in living life.

"When he came and saw the grace of God, he rejoiced."
—*Acts 11:23*

In Touch

——— ♦ ———

The eternal, continual order
of God blesses me.

If ever I am going through a challenge or a crisis, I will remember that God is my order, my peace, and my answer to prayer.

I move on with my life knowing that I am supported by a divine order that penetrates to the core of every person and situation, bringing about miraculous results. Living my life from this understanding, I recognize that a healing challenge or crisis is only temporary. The wholeness that God has created is eternal.

My recognition of divine health is a blessing for me at all times. I am in touch with the divine life that is always present so that I enjoy health, peace, and joy.

The light of divine wisdom reveals the life and healing that are there for me every day, and I accept the blessing of health and wholeness with a heart filled with gratitude to God.

> "Then God said, 'Let there be light'; and there was light. And God saw that the light was good."
> —Genesis 1:3–4

Breath of God

—◆—

*The breath of God blesses my lungs
as they perform their vital work.*

Every breath I take fills my lungs with the oxygen my
body needs to function. I am blessed as I take a few
moments to envision the miraculous process that takes
place with every breath: As I breathe in, my lungs
expand and take in vital oxygen from the air around me,
and as I exhale, carbon dioxide is released. I can almost
feel the breath of God as my lungs perform their
wondrous work.

As oxygen is conveyed from my lungs out into the
bloodstream and then throughout my body, my body is
given the nourishment it needs. My lungs are a
wonderful example of the renewal that God has
provided for me!

The breath of God blesses me each time I take a
breath. Renewed with life, I experience the joy of living.

**"My life is a breath."
—Job 7:7**

Wake-Up Call

—— ◆ ——

I answer the wake-up call to greater health
by trusting in God.

I may think of pain as anything but something positive, but I know that it is the very nature of pain to alert me that my body needs added care or a healing. It's my wake-up call to greater health.

If I am experiencing pain—from a tension headache to an upset stomach or an aching back—my body is sending a wake-up call to me that something needs to be addressed.

Immediately, I take any concern to God. Prayer takes the fear out of what I am experiencing and can even relieve the pain. I am open to divine wisdom guiding me to the best form of treatment. Perhaps I simply need to rest for a while or to make a change in the way I eat. Or I may need to seek the advice of a medical professional.

Trusting God to guide me, I answer the wake-up call to greater health.

> "He will wipe every tear from their eyes, . . .
> mourning and crying and pain will be no more."
> —Revelation 21:4

Positive Influence

—◆—

*I am dedicated to being a positive influence
of healing for my loved ones.*

Friends and loved ones are such a blessing in my life.
So whenever they are facing a health challenge, I want
to do all that I can to be a positive influence in their
healing.

I know to seek wisdom and guidance from God in
order to be a positive influence in the lives of others.
Uniting in prayer with them is something I can do to
help them along in their healing.

I also offer supportive, positive words of
encouragement to uplift their spirits. When more than
words are needed, I listen with compassion and
understanding.

I lend a helping hand by running errands for my
loved ones. Ready to be their hands and feet, I do the
tasks that they are unable to do. Being a positive
influence, I help my loved ones move forward to
renewed health.

> **"All who believed were together and
> had all things in common."
> —Acts 2:44**

Blessed Hearing

—◆—

*Through the blessing of my hearing, I am attuned
to the world in which I live.*

I may take for granted the ability to hear, but as I think about the everyday sounds that make up my world—birds singing in the morning, children laughing as they play—I give special thanks for my hearing, which helps me communicate with others.

My ears attune me to the world in which I live. With them, I am able to distinguish one sound from another and be soothed by the familiar voice of a friend or loved one. And what comfort I receive from the familiar background noises that are unique to my own life.

Yes, I am grateful for my hearing, and I bless the ears, which give me this ability. Through my blessed ears, God brings music to my life and provides a helpful tool through which I distinguish and appreciate the sounds of my world.

> "Bless our God, O peoples,
> let the sound of his praise be heard."
> —Psalms 66:8

Healing Therapy

—— ◆ ——

Music speaks a message of relaxation
and healing to me.

Soul-stirring music has been a means of soothing and uplifting people through the ages. Whether a favorite hymn, a gentle ballad, or a lively contemporary song, music conveys messages that speak to the soul.

Music speaks to my soul, too, taking my mind on a journey far away from concerns and filling me with an enthusiasm for life. The rhythm of life within me answers the call to life of the music I hear, and I am touched on a deep soul level.

My mind becomes focused on the rhythm, melody, and harmony in compositions of voices and instruments, and I become totally absorbed in the music I hear.

Music serves as a kind of healing therapy for my mind and body. I feel so uplifted and inspired that my body is energized and renewed.

"I will give them one heart, and put
a new spirit within them."
—Ezekiel 11:19

Loving Pets

———◆———

*Thank God for pets that teach me how
to love unconditionally.*

Those who have taught me my most meaningful lessons in life have not always been people with teaching degrees. Sometimes they have not been people at all.

The eager, unrestrained affection of a pet has lifted me out of sadness and disappointment that I couldn't seem to shake by myself. It's as if the wagging of the tail, the licks of affection, and the purrs of delight are telling me, "God loves you, and I love you, too! So how could you possibly be sad?"

My pets look to me for food and water and affection. However, they are willing to give me so much more. I believe they are teaching me about unconditional love and acceptance as they walk with me on the path of life, giving and receiving love.

> "He will feed his flock like a shepherd;
> he will gather the lambs in his arms,
> and carry them in his bosom,
> and gently lead the mother sheep."
> —Isaiah 40:11

Sense of Humor

———◆———

*My sense of humor blesses me with
a positive, lighthearted approach to life.*

Given a little time, I realize that some of my most
embarrassing moments are now memories that cause
me to smile or even laugh. Oh, how much more
enjoyable my memories become when I let my sense of
humor shine on them.

Maybe what I am sensing is this: A lighthearted
approach to mistakes or flubs is really divine wisdom
telling me that I am not a failure even though I did not
achieve what I wanted to achieve.

This divine, lighthearted approach helps me in the
midst of challenge. So what if I say something wrong or
do something awkward in front of others? When I
smile, make a lighthearted comment, and go on with
what I am doing, I put myself and those around me at
ease. My sense of humor gives me greater
understanding. It keeps me feeling positive about life
and ready to experience all that's ahead.

> "This is the day that the Lord has made;
> let us rejoice and be glad in it."
> —Psalms 118:24

Meditation

—◆—

"My heart is steadfast, O God,
my heart is steadfast."
—Psalms 108:1

Becoming quiet, I envision how my heart works
tirelessly for me:

With a strong and steady beat, my heart
pumps nourishment throughout my body to every
muscle and fiber of my being.

Day after day, year after year, my heart
continues its vital role, working in partnership with
the other organs in my body to ensure a quality life
for me.

I bless my heart and give thanks for its life-
sustaining beat. What a marvelous example of
God's artistic genius my heart is!

I give thanks that my heart is a constant
reminder of God's love for me. I envision my heart
performing its unending activity, sending wave
after wave of love throughout my body.

My heart is a beautiful symbol of the love I
have for others—a love from God that is steadfast
and strong, a love that is expressed by me to others.

DAILY WORD FOR HEALING

Prayer

—◆—

*"Pray for us as well that God will open
to us a door for the word, that we
may declare the mystery of Christ."*
—Colossians 4:3

Dear God, what relief I feel when I set aside my
own expectations and let divine love be my
inspiration as I pray for a healing. I am placing my
self in Your tender care. My complete trust is in
You, God, not on circumstances or conditions. I
know that You are the life that renews me with
energy, and You will guide me through every
decision I make.

I declare, dear God, that I am open and
receptive to healing. With an awareness of Your
presence within me, I know that I am worthy of a
life of health and well-being.

God, through Your presence within me, I am
healed. It is on the road of life and recovery that I
envision myself—now and always.

Listen, Beloved

—◆—

Beloved,

If you are feeling shaken because you are going through a severe health challenge, trust in Me and I will give you the hope and reassurance you need.

Remember that I am always with you—even when the dawn seems long in coming and fears are overwhelming your mind and heart.

The peace you seek is closer to you than the air you breathe and the thoughts you think, for I am the life and peace that indwell you, now and eternally. My presence surrounds you, so open your heart and mind to Me and be at peace.

No matter where you may be, I will answer when you call Me, for we can never be apart.

I am the life that enlivens you—part of all that you are and ever will be. Be at peace, beloved child, for you and I are one, now and forever.

> *"When you search for me,*
> *you will find me."*
> *—Jeremiah 29:13*

Divine Image

—◆—

God loves me just as I am, and God's love is
my inspiration for looking and feeling healthy and fit.

Am I feeling some anguish about my physical appearance because of someone's opinion of how I should look? Then I remind myself that God loves and accepts me just as I am.

In the silence of my soul, God speaks to me with loving words and reminds me that I have been created in the divine image. God assures me that whether I am considered tall or short, heavy or thin, it is the condition of my soul that is important.

Feeling positive about myself just naturally shows in my outer appearance. I love and respect myself for who I am: a child of God. With the help of my Creator, I will be guided to the proper foods to eat and the right exercise I need to keep my body fit.

I come away from my time of prayer with the blessed assurance that above all else, God will always love me just as I am.

"And all of us, . . . seeing the glory of the Lord as
though reflected in a mirror, are being transformed into
the same image from one degree of glory to another."
—2 Corinthians 3:18

I Care!

———◆———

I am a loving individual who cares about
and for my loved ones.

I have made many decisions throughout my life. Most concerned my own health and well-being, but some were decisions that affected my loved ones as well.

I care for my family and friends and want to do what is best for them. So when I am making decisions about my own care or if I am being a caregiver for my family, I turn to God for guidance. With God guiding me, I am assured that the decisions I make are inspired by spiritual understanding. God has blessed me with a generous heart and the capacity to fill my heart with an unlimited amount of love.

I pray about all matters that concern my own well-being or the well-being of my family and friends. Because I care enough to want the highest good for my family and friends, I pray for them and I pray to be a blessing to them.

> "Without ceasing I remember you
> always in my prayers."
> —Romans 1:9

Journey to Peace

——◆——

*God comforts me and instills me
with hope.*

One of the hardest things I may ever have to do after
suffering a loss is to pick up the pieces of my life and
move on. Although I may not have a physical ailment,
my heart needs time to recuperate.

God is my hope. God is the light that shines within
me and soothes my weary heart. Whatever my need,
God is there—my source of comfort and strength and
courage to look toward the future.

As hard as it may be for me to believe at the time,
God will fill the void caused by what I have lost, and
my heart will be healed. If I feel lost, I look within my
heart and let God guide me in taking the next step.

With every step I take, God is right there with me,
giving me strength and inspiring me with hope to begin
my journey back to peace of mind and heart.

"Now may our Lord Jesus Christ himself and God our
Father, who loved us and through grace gave us eternal
comfort and good hope, comfort your hearts
and strengthen them in every good work and word."
—2 Thessalonians 2:16–17

I Am Patient

———◆———

Being patient is a way I express my love for life.

I love life and I know that my love for life helps me be patient with myself and others. Life is so much more meaningful and interesting when I practice patience. Being patient is a way of practicing good health.

I think about how much stress I save my body from going through when I am patient: Even when the service is slow at a restaurant, I remain calm while I'm waiting to be served. Then, once my food arrives, I am able to enjoy eating it and also able to digest my food well. Being patient, I have saved myself from stomach upset.

Because I am patient with myself and others in my home and workplace, I think clearly. I keep myself from feeling stressed and from adding to the pressure others might be experiencing. Avoiding feelings of stress, I help regulate my own blood pressure.

I truly love the life that God has given me, and being patient is a way I express that love.

"Love is patient."
—1 Corinthians 13:4

Nurturing Strength

—◆—

*God is my strength
and my comfort.*

For children who are afraid of the dark, hugs and words of comfort from Mom and Dad can bring instant reassurance.

As a child of God, it is calming for me to know that whenever I need comfort, God will nurture me and reassure me.

At any time of the day or night, I can move beyond fear and concern about my well-being to knowing that I am in the presence of God. Then I feel the soothing love of God surrounding and calming me.

As a loving parent, God is always ready to comfort and strengthen me. God is my life and my all.

The presence of God is forever an inseparable part of who I am and how I came to be.

"How precious is your steadfast love, O God!
All people may take refuge in the shadow
of your wings."
—Psalms 36:7

Understanding

—◆—

God blesses me with wisdom
and understanding.

I look to God's light of understanding within me to guide me through any time of decision.

Then I know that I will know when to refrain from speaking and acting and when to move forward with confidence to question and make changes in my health routine.

The certain and absolute knowledge that God's presence and wisdom are within me saves me from taking a wrong turn in life. I take the direct ways and turns that lead me toward my goal of greater health.

I thank God for keeping me from wandering in the desert of confusion. God's tender mercy enfolds me and strengthens me. The light of God's wisdom radiates out from me in crises and everyday matters.

Oh, how greatly God blesses me!

"By the tender mercy of our God,
the dawn from on high will break upon us."
—Luke 1:78

Winds of Change

———◆———

God is with me through
every change in life.

I have arrived at this time and place by divine appointment. I know that I can never be without God's loving presence. God is with me as I end one chapter of my life and begin a new one.

I understand that changes can occur as gently as a breeze whispering through the trees or as swiftly and unpredictably as a gathering storm bursting upon the scene. Whether a physical, financial, or personal change comes gradually or quickly, I know that God is supporting me through all the turning points of my life.

God is the one constant in my life. Though the winds of change may blow, I will never fear them or what they may bring. God's presence fills me with the hope and strength to go through any change.

"I am about to do a new thing; now it springs forth,
do you not perceive it?"
—Isaiah 43:19

Mobility

—◆—

*God has created me
to be healthy and whole.*

Granted, my joints and muscles may not enable me to be as flexible or as limber as I was when I was a child, but thank God that divine life in me is continually rejuvenating me and keeping me mobile. If, on occasion, my joints should ache because of overexertion or everyday stress or strain, I know one of the best remedies is prayer.

"Dear God, thank You for this body that continues to serve me daily. Bless my arms and legs and keep them free from pain.

"I see myself walking and running with ease of movement, and I visualize my fingers and thumbs grasping and lifting the things that I require them to. Such imagery sends a message of life and vitality to every joint and muscle of my body.

"I am as You created me to be, O God—healthy and whole."

> "Cast your burden on the Lord,
> and he will sustain you."
> —Psalms 55:22

HOW DREAMS COME TRUE
BY LARRY MOORE

W hen I look back, the irony of it all continues to emerge. As a TV anchorperson and a member of the Dream Factory, a nonprofit organization that fulfills the wishes of terminally or seriously ill children, I had held back my emotions as I worked with the news and children every day. Yet the thing that got me started on the road to healing was one of the very things I had held back: my tears.

About 6 years ago, a small bump appeared just under my right eye, but I didn't give it much thought. However, when tears began to stream down the corner of that same eye for no apparent reason, my wife, Ruth, encouraged me to see a doctor. And I did—without her having to nag me about it.

One of the first things the doctor prescribed was 48 hours of a high-powered antibiotic. His instructions were, "Come back in 2 days," and again I didn't hesitate to do just as he said. After 2 days the bump was still there, so we knew it was not a simple infection. Several other causes were eliminated, and the final diagnosis came as a shock to me: I had a malignant tumor. It was still treatable with high-powered chemotherapy drugs and radiation, but the doctor explained that if I had waited even 30 days

DAILY WORD FOR HEALING

longer, the cancer would have spread throughout my body.

I think it was at this point that I knew without a doubt I was being divinely guided. Sure I had listened to my wife and my doctor—not putting off an appointment for a few days or a few months—but there was something greater than any of us guiding me through to a healing. I knew this was true.

Ruth and I decided that we might do some good for others if I went public with my condition. So with the support of my family, the general manager of the TV station, and my coworkers, I told the television audience I had cancer and that my appearance might change because I was going through chemotherapy and radiation.

Immediately, the letters and calls began to pour in. The faith support was overwhelming. I received 2,500 letters from viewers. Several were from Dream Factory children. Some I had met years ago, and they were now in college or married with children of their own. They were survivors, and I would be too!

One letter in particular touched me. It was from a child whom I had recently met through the Dream Factory. She had undergone chemotherapy. She wrote, "Mr. Moore, I will love you even when you lose all your hair." Her message gave new meaning to a popular saying: "Been there; done that."

My wife and children stood by me, and I needed

DAILY WORD FOR HEALING

them to lean on—physically at times—for support. My boss assured me, "We'll get through this together." My coworkers filled in for me when all I could do was come to the station, read the news, and then go home to bed.

I won't say that cancer treatment is easy, but I will say that it was made easier by what I call My Recipe for the Cure of Cancer: Start with early detection; add a heaping portion of faith (yours and that of all who are willing to share); pour in a large measure of the support of family and friends.

I'm back to full strength now. Sometimes I work up to 40 hours a week as a member of the Dream Factory—beyond my regular job as a news anchor. When I meet with the children now, I have a new understanding of how one person's faith can be added to another's.

So I feel I help bring each child more than a dream—a trip to Disney World or a new computer—I also bring a faith that believes in the best for them. Right now, I can't think of a better dream come true than that.

Loving Environment

———◆———

*I help create the loving environment
in which I thrive.*

When I am trying to get past a difficult situation, I find that a positive perspective makes it easier for me to get on with my life and to be healthy. I remember that when people seem harsh or uncaring, it is their words and actions that I dislike—not the people themselves.

All humankind share the common bond of spiritual kinship, and I respect all people because they are children of God. From this perspective, I focus my attention on positive thoughts about the people I interact with. I give them and the situations we are involved in my prayerful attention.

Prayer is the key to finding answers to the questions on my mind. When my question is whether to forgive, I know that God's answer will be *yes*. God is pure, unconditional love. Because I am created by Love, I thrive in a loving environment—an environment I help to create.

"Beloved, we are God's children now."
—1 John 3:2

Exercise

—— ◆ ——

*The life of God fills me with energy and inspires me
so that I exercise my body wisely.*

There may be some mornings when it is an effort just
to get out of bed, let alone find the energy to exercise.
Yet I know that because the spirit of God is within me, I
have a reservoir of energy to call upon.

Exercise is vitally important to the overall health of
my body. It tones not only the muscles I am using but
also the very cells and organs of my body. A walk
improves my circulation and increases the breathing
capacity of my lungs. As I exercise, I encourage each cell
to work more efficiently as it eliminates toxins and
waste matter.

There are so many options available in the way that I
exercise! Whether I enjoy a brisk walk in the morning or
a more intense workout during the day, I pick a routine
that I find enjoyable. Then I will have the motivation to
stick with my program, and I will find greater
enjoyment in giving my body the exercise it needs.

"Awake, my soul!"
—Psalms 57:8

Creative Activities

—◆—

My hobbies are creative activities that improve
my physical and mental well-being.

I have a creative spirit, and I use hobbies as an outlet for my creativity. When I truly enjoy what I am doing, whether it involves a craft, sports, music, or art, I reap wonderful benefits.

Allowing myself to become totally focused on a hobby is a great way to keep my mind clear of worry thoughts. The enjoyment I receive from what I am doing frees me to direct positive, creative energy toward doing it. A sense of peace enfolds me as I concentrate.

There are physical benefits as well. A leisurely hobby allows me to spend time in a relaxed, restful state. An hour or so of doing something for the pure joy it brings me melts any tension from my body. I am calm and serene.

If I am involved in sports such as volleyball or bowling, I feel invigorated as my muscles and organs perform at such a high level, giving a boost to my whole body. I feel great!

"A cheerful heart has a continual feast."
—Proverbs 15:15

Memory

—◆—

*I remember all that I need to remember
when I need to remember it.*

If I have forgotten where I put my car keys or what ingredients to use in a favorite recipe, I may become mildly irritated. Not being able to think of the name of someone I have known for years or not knowing the answer to a test question, however, may cause me to be seriously upset.

A lapse in memory would make anyone nervous, but there is a way to overcome any doubt I may have about the state of my mind. In any time of confusion, I can calm myself by taking my mind off the situation and turning my attention to the presence of God within me.

In silence with God, I release worry and stress and open my mind to the inspiration of Spirit. Then God reveals what I need to know. With poise and self-assurance, I remember what I need to know when I need to know it.

> **"Those who are spiritual discern all things, and they
> are themselves subject to no one else's scrutiny. . . .
> We have the mind of Christ."
> —1 Corinthians 2:15–16**

TODAY'S MESSAGE:
Living My Belief

—◆—

*I am living my belief in
the miracle-working power of God!*

Several times when people in need approached Jesus,
He asked, "Do you believe?" (Mark 9:28). With a
question, He was teaching them that they had an active
part to play in their own healing and understanding of
spiritual principles.

It is true: I am living my beliefs each day. Because I
believe I can overcome a dependency, experience a
healing, or accomplish a dream, I can! Spending time in
prayer moves me past limiting thoughts to the
unlimited power of God within me.

I am living my faith; I believe in and live from the
presence of God within me. My response to every
challenge is a powerful declaration of faith: *I believe
in God!*

"'Do you believe that I am able to do this?' They said
to him, 'Yes, Lord.' Then he touched their eyes
and said, 'According to your faith let it be done to you.'
And their eyes were opened."
—Matthew 9:28–30

Seasons of Life

——— ◆ ———

*I give expression to the life of God within me
in every season of my life.*

I might view life as a series of different seasons. The
early season of life is one of intense physical growth
and learning. The midseason is ripe with planning and
looking ahead. Although the later season may contain
reflection, it is still rich with growth and learning, with
planning and looking forward.

With each new season, I am willing to experience
more of life. I bring the best of each year, each season
with me into a new time of exploration and discovery.

Whatever the season of my life, I never want to
forget how important the development of my spiritual
awareness is. I am an eternal spiritual being living a
human experience. I know this because I am aware of
God's spirit at the core of my being. Each season is
important and fulfilling because it is an opportunity for
me to experience and express the presence of God.

> "For everything there is a season, and a time
> for every matter under heaven."
> —Ecclesiastes 3:1

Work Blessing

—— ◆ ——

I am blessed as I bless others
through my work.

What is it I want from my job or career? Financial security would be high on the list, but even more important is a feeling of fulfillment in whatever I do.

So in doing my current work or in looking for a new job or in seeking a promotion, I make a commitment to God:

"God, help me so that the work I do will help others and also bring me true satisfaction. I want to bless people and bring greater comfort to them. Sometimes You let me know that my blessing to others is my compassion toward them. Other times You give me knowledge that brings greater efficiency and productivity to my workplace.

"Whatever is mine to do, God, I am willing to do. I am blessed as I bless others, and blessings come back to me multiplied."

> **"Commit your work to the Lord,**
> **and your plans will be established."**
> **—Proverbs 16:3**

Nourishing Life

— ◆ —

*I eat wisely and enjoy
what I eat.*

Eating too much or too little can become a habit that grows into a problem. And feeling guilty about the way I eat will only add to my frustration.

So I pray about what and how I eat. I pray to fully realize that food is the fuel that energizes me and to take in the right amount of fuel. When I eat, I take in the amount I need for strength and vitality.

I pray before I eat—every time I eat. I do this to bring more prayer into my day and to think about what I am about to eat. Choosing an apple instead of potato chips feels right for me. And the apple tastes so good after I've prayed: "Thank you, God, for this crisp, red apple that grew from a beautiful tree."

Eating is a part of everyday life. Like the breath of life, the food of life is essential to me. I eat wisely and enjoy what I eat.

**"He took the seven loaves and the fish; and after giving
thanks he broke them and gave them to the disciples. . . .
And all of them ate and were filled."
—Matthew 15:36–37**

Meditation

—◆—

*"I will cause breath to enter you,
and you shall live."*
—Ezekiel 37:5

In the solitude of prayer, I give thanks for my lungs
and the vital function they perform in maintaining
good health.

As I breathe in, my lungs take in the oxygen
my body needs to produce healthy blood and cells.
So I bless my lungs and envision them healthy and
whole.

I do all that I can to help my lungs function
properly by breathing deeply and allowing each
breath to fill my lungs completely. As I exhale, I hold
a vision of myself releasing what my body no longer
needs so that I am refreshed by my next breath.

If I have adopted habits that I know are not
healthy for my lungs, I ask God for guidance and
strength in releasing those habits and leaving them
behind. God will show me what I need to do.

My lungs continue their important work
whether I am awake or asleep, and I am so very
grateful for my lungs and the incredible renewing
work they do.

DAILY WORD FOR HEALING

Prayer

—◆—

*"Jumping up, he stood and began
to walk, and he entered the temple with them,
walking and leaping and praising God."*
—Acts 3:8

God, in this very moment, I claim a healing from anything that is coming between me and my total well-being. I claim a healing through Your spirit within me, which is constantly renewing me cell by cell, breath by breath, heartbeat by heartbeat.

In this very moment, I celebrate a healing— even before I see or feel any improvement in myself. My gratitude to You builds an enthusiasm for life that helps heal my mind and body.

God, it is Your spirit of life within me that heals me. I am refreshed by an energy that surges throughout my body in a healing flow of divine life and love. I am alive with divine life that awakens me to both the wholeness of my physical body and the holiness of my spiritual identity. I feel Your joy and peace filling me with strength as I gratefully affirm, "I am healed!"

Listen, Beloved

—◆—

Beloved,

Lean on Me. In all your times of need, through every experience of your life, I am with you to support you with love and understanding.

I am your comfort and strength. When you feel as if you cannot stand on your own, lean on Me and let My love for you sustain you through and past every doubt and fear.

No matter what you do, beloved, I will always love you. No matter where you go, I will be there. Through every moment of the day and night, through every moment of crisis or achievement, I am with you. I am holding you in My tender embrace.

If you need courage or strength, lean on Me. When you need comfort and faith, I am here. You can rely on Me, beloved, for I have breathed the breath of life into you and sustain you in every moment of life. Never forget that with you, I am well pleased.

"This is my Son, the Beloved,
with whom I am well pleased."
—Matthew 3:17

DAILY WORD FOR HEALING

Divine Plan

— ◆ —

*I listen to and follow
God's plan for me.*

One of the greatest resources I have is my God-given ability to make sound judgments. By listening to God, I am able to understand what is in my best interest and what ensures my well-being.

God has given me life, and I am grateful for that life. With a deep and abiding faith in God, I never take any blessing for granted. The blessing of God's guidance includes my instant and constant access to a divine plan that guides me in making decisions about my own welfare.

I know that God cares about and for me. When situations present themselves that seem more like challenges than opportunities, I realize that although I may not have all the answers, God does.

With a trusting heart, I turn to God in prayer. Then I listen to and follow a divine plan.

> "In God, whose word I praise,
> in God I trust; I am not afraid."
> —Psalms 56:4

Prevention

——◆——

Prayer, exercise, and proper nutrition are preventive measures that help me stay healthy.

My everyday choices and actions help me avoid being in harmful or dangerous situations. I can also use preventive measures to remain whole and well.

I begin with prayer. My body and the precious gift of life I have been given are from God, so I naturally turn to my Creator when seeking guidance about what is good for my body and in my life.

I then understand that I need to eat a healthy balance of nutritional, substantial foods. I am committed to following a routine of exercise so that my heart and muscles remain strong. I make an investment in continued good health by having regular checkups.

I experience such peace of mind knowing that I am cooperating with God concerning my own health and wholeness.

> "The light of the eyes rejoices the heart,
> and good news refreshes the body."
> —Proverbs 15:30

Absolute Wisdom

—◆—

*With every decision I make, I turn
to God for guidance.*

Because my family and friends love and care about me
and want me to be healthy and whole, they may feel
compelled to offer me advice about my health. I know
they mean well, so I thank them for their good
intentions. But the One I turn to for the guidance I need
in making a decision is God.

I pray that I have the understanding and prayer
support of my loved ones. I affirm that God is life and
wisdom being expressed by me. How blessed I am
knowing that divine life is constantly healing me and
restoring my mind and body to wholeness. As I pray, I
bless my body for the work that it does and feel a
divine response. As I continue my journey of health and
wholeness, I am moving forward in faith.

From the seemingly insignificant decisions to those
that will ultimately change the course of my life, I
always turn to God.

"Lead me in your truth, and teach me."
—Psalms 25:5

A New Dawn

———◆———

I trust God.

During the darkest hours of a challenge, I may feel as if it will take a miracle to bring light back into my life. Yet I know that the dark of night is only the prelude to the beginning of a new day and the return of warmth and brightness.

I know this is true because God has created a world of order and balance. I trust God's order to provide a balance of night and day, of rest and renewal for all life on Earth—including me.

So when events in my life look hopeless, I have faith that a new dawn will come—a new day of endless possibilities.

My faith is in God. Even when I cannot see the bigger picture—why something is happening—I trust God to guide me each step of the way. I know that God will not fail to restore order and balance to my life.

> "Through him you have come to trust
> in God, who . . . gave him glory, so that
> your faith and hope are set on God."
> —1 Peter 1:21

Partnership with God

——— ◆ ———

I live my life in partnership with God. Together we are building a healthy, fulfilling life.

Day by day, I am building my life on a foundation that God has created for me.

The life-affirming thoughts I think and the choices I make are the tools I use in shaping a life of meaning and purpose.

I am building a life that is rich with meaning and purpose. The choices I make are ones that are inclusive and embrace life with the joy of living.

What an honor it is to be in partnership with God as I make simple decisions and life-changing resolutions! Knowing that I am living my life in partnership with God, I make choices that are the building blocks on a foundation that lead to a healthy, fulfilling life.

"According to the grace of God given to me,
like a skilled master builder I laid a foundation,
and someone else is building on it. Each builder
must choose with care how to build on it."
—1 Corinthians 3:10

Prayer of Faith

—◆—

In prayer, I remember that God is always with me—
restoring me and keeping me whole.

I begin to pray with an understanding of the purpose
and meaning of all my prayers: "God, I realize that in
prayer I am not calling You to me; rather, I am
remembering that You are always with me."

Then I continue to pray, fully aware that the spirit of
God is within me: "God, You are my true reality. Your
loving, living spirit moves through me, restoring my
mind and body. Your presence is a beacon of love and
life that shines brightly from within me.

"Yes, God, You are always with me as a healing and
revealing presence of life and wisdom. My 'amen' is not
an end to my conversation with You; it is my
commitment to bring an awareness of You to every
moment of this day."

> "Trust in the Lord forever,
> for in the Lord God
> you have an everlasting rock."
> —Isaiah 26:4

I Value God's World

———◆———

God placed me in a world
of abundance and wonder.

What I value most are those blessings on which no material value can be placed: being aware of the life and love of God around me, interacting with the people I love and who love me, living the experiences that move me beyond the limits of what I had once thought I could do, and knowing that God cares about me and for me in every moment of life.

The kingdom of God, the realm of divine ideas, is my prosperity. I not only think, I invite God to think divine thoughts through me. I act from my own understanding of what will benefit me and others and open my life to God so that blessings will occur through me.

How prosperous I feel when I am aware that I live in a world created by God—a virtual panorama of abundance and wonder.

"To keep understanding is to prosper."
—Proverbs 19:8

New Heights

—◆—

As an expression of God,
I am free in spirit.

Watching an eagle soar effortlessly on the wind, I may wonder how such freedom would feel. If only I were able to stretch out my arms and catch the wind, I, too, would no longer be earthbound. Yet I know that such freedom is temporary and conditional, for the eagle must return to earth.

There is a greater freedom, a glorious uplifting of the spirit that frees me to soar to new heights. I am more than a physical being—I am a spiritual being, an expression of God. I am capable of soaring as long as I do not tether myself to any preconceived ideas of limitation or dependency. I dare to follow my dreams, for through God's spirit within, I am unlimited.

As I watch the eagle soar, gracefully gliding through the air, I declare for myself: "Yes, I can! I can soar above limitations, for I am free in spirit!"

"'Who is he, sir? Tell me, so that I may believe in him.'
Jesus said to him, 'You have seen him, and the
one speaking with you is he.' He said, 'Lord, I believe.'"
—John 9:36–38

Meditation

———◆———

"God, who knows the human heart, testified to them by giving them the Holy Spirit . . . and in cleansing their hearts by faith he has made no distinction between them and us."—Acts 15:8–9

As I sit in silence, a time of sacred reverence, I relax and let go of any thought that does not affirm health and wholeness.

I put aside concerns about health challenges and the possible outcomes and focus totally on God. Breathing in, I visualize a healing flow of life moving throughout my body and then enfolding me. Completely relaxed and with my mind at ease, I know I am in God's holy presence.

In silence with God, I put aside my own list of wants and simply listen. God speaks to me as joy and acceptance, understanding and forgiveness— and all else that is important for me to live a healthy life.

Each thought and prayer prompts a cleansing and renewing within my body. As the cells and tissues of my body respond with renewed health, I understand that no condition is greater than God's power to heal.

Prayer

*"But as for me,
I will look to the Lord."
—Micah 7:7*

God, how refreshed I feel when I release worry and doubt and give everything over to You for a divine solution. I realize that as I free my mind of fear and concern, I open myself to healing.

Whenever I let go and let You be the main focus of my thoughts and activities, I am being an active partner with You in creating a life of wonder. I see challenges as opportunities to learn and stretch beyond limitations that I myself or others have placed on me.

Life is not always easy, God, but knowing that You are with me every moment and throughout every day instills me with hope. The challenges I encounter may be small or monumental, but I overcome each one as I cooperate with You. As Your faith-filled partner, God, I open my mind and body to Your healing presence.

Listen, Beloved

—— ◆ ——

Beloved,

I am the wisdom that surpasses the understanding of the ages, the order that rules the universe, and the love that will carry you through every experience.

My love gives form and substance to you and to all else that I have created.

I am the comfort you feel when you turn within. I am the peace that causes your heart to sing with joy and your spirit to soar to new heights of awareness.

Look and you will see Me in the faces of your loved ones as glowing expressions of My presence. Listen and you will hear Me in the laughter of children that dances upon the air as a gentle reminder of My love for all.

I am all that you will ever need. I am with you always—in times of crisis and celebration and all times in between.

"God said to Moses, 'I am who I am.' He said further, 'Thus you shall say to the Israelites, "I am has sent me to you."'"
—Exodus 3:14

My Prayer

— ◆ —

*Here I am, God; guide me in being blessed
and in blessing others.*

My prayer is to be on my right path in life. I know that
when I am following the guidance of my Creator, I will
meet divine appointments with people, experiences,
and situations—all of which will bless me and which I
will bless.

"Dear God, here I am, Your willing child. Lead me
on paths that will bring to me the light of compassion
and understanding. Knowing You are my constant
companion, I have courage that is built on my faith
in You.

"Wherever I am, You are with me. Whatever I
experience, You are there to encourage and guide me.
Every step I take, I am moving from and onto holy
ground, for Your spirit is everywhere.

"God, You are my life, my breath, my vision. I will
follow where You lead me, moving forward and taking
with me a realization of Your presence and power."

**"And there will be no more night; they need no light
of lamp or sun, for the Lord God will be their light."
—Revelation 22:5**

In Motion

— ◆ —

*I give thanks to God for my ability
to move and stretch effortlessly.*

I may not think about how important it is for me to
listen to my body until my hips or knees start talking to
me through aches and pains. Translated into words,
their message may be that I need to give them a rest and
to refrain from overusing them.

What a marvelous plan God carried out in giving my
body support, strength, and mobility through the
network of joints in my body. I bless my joints in
prayer, and I use good judgment in how I can help them
function at their best.

I may choose to walk briskly instead of run so that I
don't cause harsh impact to my knee and hip joints. I
stretch to keep the range of motion of my shoulders at
an optimum. Best of all, I give thanks to God for my
mobility. In a flow of gratitude, my words of
thanksgiving move through me to bless my whole body.

> "It is not you that support the root,
> but the root that supports you."
> —Romans 11:18

An Overcoming Spirit

——— ◆ ———

God is showing me a new way
of life and a better future.

I am a child of God. The spirit of God that lives within me infuses me with light and love and a freedom of Spirit that enables me to overcome any challenge or dependency.

So if I have adopted a habit or style of living that I know is not good for my health and well-being, I turn to that indwelling spirit of God for help. I call on God's strength to strengthen me and invite divine wisdom to lead me forward, leaving the negative habit or lifestyle in the past.

It is not always easy to follow a new path that might take me away from what is familiar, yet I know that God is with me and provides all the strength and courage I need to face each challenge as it comes.

Free with the freedom of Spirit, I thank God for showing me a new way of life and a brighter future!

> "Do you not know that you are God's temple
> and that God's Spirit dwells in you?"
> —1 Corinthians 3:16

Vision of God's World

———◆———

*I see that the presence of God
is everywhere.*

I thank God for the colorful, spectacular images that I
am able to see. Vision stimulates my mind and gives me
information about my surroundings.

Yet there is infinitely more activity going on in my
own backyard than my eyes can possibly show me.
When I see bees collecting nectar from flowers, do I
recognize more than a beautiful image of nature? Do I
also feel a gladness of heart because I have done my
part in a divine plan of life? It's true: I planted the seed,
the seed grew into flowers, and the bees are doing their
part by collecting nectar to make honey.

My eyes give me views of God's world—views that I
take into my thoughts and my heart. As I give thanks
for my eyes and bless them in prayer, I am opening
them to the beauty and inspiration of God's creativity. I
am seeing with my eyes and also with my heart and my
soul that the presence of God is everywhere.

"Their eyes see every precious thing."
—Job 28:10

Change

———◆———

God is with me, supporting me and encouraging me through all times of change.

At times, even the thought of having to make a change in my routine or having to learn something new may cause me to feel anxious.

When I take a deep breath and calm down, however, I realize that change is inevitable: new inventions and technology are constantly bringing change and progress to daily living. These changes are a blessing to me and to others.

In every moment of my life, God is with me to support and encourage me through any kind of change. God presents me with opportunities to grow and to develop, which in turn enable me to move beyond my hopes and make them realities.

I am more than a mere creature of habit. I am a spiritual being capable of learning more and moving beyond my accomplishments to even greater ones.

> "God is the strength of my heart
> and my portion forever."
> —Psalms 73:26

Spirit Reaching Out

———◆———

*My faith assures me of God's presence
in me and my loved ones.*

Whenever I am concerned about my own health or in doubt about a healing, I ask myself this question: "If my faith is a belief in God, how could I not have faith?"

This simple question gets me focused on where my faith needs to be—in God. The presence of God is within me, within others, and within all conditions and circumstances, so my prayer is for all of us to be willing to let God work through us:

"God, I do have faith in You. As I open my mind and heart and life to You, marvelous happenings occur. I know that I will be healed because You are a healing presence within me.

"I have faith in You, God, for Your spirit reaches out through me, other people, and the events of today. My faith is a palpable vote of confidence in Your presence and power within me and others."

> **"He said to her, 'Daughter, your faith
> has made you well; go in peace.'"
> —Luke 8:48**

God Values Me

———◆———

God values me.

God is my all; therefore, I have all I need to be healthy in mind and body, to be fulfilled emotionally and spiritually.

In my times of prayer, God speaks to me with words of reassurance:

"Dear one, I have made you in My image. You are a priceless treasure, and the love and kindness you bring to the world are of tremendous value. You are a reflection of My light and My eternal love.

"Your contributions to the world may not seem monumental, but within you lies the power to brighten the life of another with your smiles, hugs, and kind words. You are an invaluable masterpiece that I have created, and I love you."

As God speaks to me, I feel divine love embracing me, and I come away from my time of prayer with a renewed sense of value.

**"Consider the ravens: They neither sow nor reap, they have neither storehouse nor barn, and yet God feeds them. Of how much more value are you than the birds!"
—Luke 12:24**

Gentle Reassurance

———◆———

With gentle reassurance,
God comforts me.

In some areas of the world, all of nature prepares for the arrival of winter. Silently falling snow will cover the bare ground. The surface of the ground reflects anything but abundant life.

Yet underneath the soil, within the roots of the plants that have shed their leaves and within the hearts of the various animals that are hibernating, vibrant life is present.

If, in my own life, appearances seem less than ideal, I know that within my soul is a sacred place where the presence of God abides. No person or event can harm my soul, for it is nurtured and protected by the spirit of God.

Within my soul, I find the comfort I seek. I rest in silence and I am strengthened by being totally in the presence of God. With gentle reassurance, God comforts me and assures me that all is well.

"The Lord lives! Blessed be my rock,
and exalted be the God of my salvation."
—Psalms 18:46

Yes, God, I Can!
By Bonnie St. John Deane

During my growing-up years, I lived my life in a mental landscape that I created for myself. In my imagination, I was a strong and graceful runner. I was beautiful and popular, and I could be anything that I wanted to be.

In reality, I had been born with a stunted right leg. My left leg was fully developed and continued to grow, but my right leg was extremely underdeveloped and short. I was unable to walk normally until I was 6 years old—after I had had surgeries to stiffen my knee so that it wouldn't bend and to remove my right foot so I could be fitted with an artificial leg.

Living in my imaginary world, I was able to control my thoughts and feelings while I was awake, but during the nights in the hospital, I would scream out in my sleep. A nurse would come to wake me from the nightmares so I could go back to sleep.

Much later in life, I understood what had caused the nightmares. It was only after my stepfather died when I was 18 that I allowed myself to remember that he had molested me. Feeling so much emotional pain and trauma during my early years, I had stuffed the memories of abuse into the darkest corners of my mind.

DAILY WORD FOR HEALING

I escaped the pain through reading and through living in my imagination. I read books at night after everybody else was asleep. I shut myself in the bathroom, turned on the light, and read on the floor. I read in the car and on the playground while other kids jumped rope and played kickball.

When I was 8 years old, my mother gave me a brochure. On the cover was a silhouette of an amputee skier with this headline: "If I can do this, I can do anything!" I didn't realize it then, but the amputee pictured on the cover was showing me what I would someday be able to do.

In junior high school, I didn't feel popular or attractive. I wasn't good in sports, and I was always the last person picked when teams were chosen. The prayer chapel in the Episcopal school I attended became my sanctuary.

I was around 15 when a friend invited me to go skiing with her and her family. She was kind and upbeat, never questioning that her one-legged friend could ski. This friend changed my life.

Resolving to step out of the mental landscape I was creating with my imagination, I began to live in the real world. I wanted to ski! When I first started, I lacked balance and strength, so I leaned over my heavy outrigger ski poles. I tried to race using regular poles, but I kept falling.

Finally, I threw aside my ski poles, went to the bunny hill, and learned how to ski with nothing in my hands.

Learning how to ski with just one ski and no poles, I gained a tremendous amount of strength and balance. Then I was able to ski with poles, planting them in the snow so that I could pop up in the air and twist. This was a very exhilarating, free way to ski. In competition, I had to use outriggers, but I learned that they were not a crutch; they were incredible tools that helped me go all the way to the Olympics and win.

The joy and passion I felt while training for the Olympics helped me to discover my spiritual strengths, too. At times, I had felt as if I were using prayer as a crutch. Then, as I began to reach out more and more to God, I understood that prayer is an incredible tool that helped me to heal, but that I had some work to do myself. Just as I had to learn to work with the outriggers instead of leaning on them, I learned to work with divine power instead of leaning on God.

I have a wonderful husband now and a precious daughter, but when she turned 4—the same age I was when I was molested—many painful memories came back to haunt me. There were times when I felt so down, all I could do was just sit and cry. The love I felt from knowing the presence of God is the only thing that pulled me back up.

I could have let those destructive memories and the emotions ruin me and my family, but I began to release them. I went to God in prayer, and God strengthened me so that I could heal.

I am making progress in my recovery, but I still have a way to go. The memories I have experienced in the last couple of years have been more difficult than anything else I have ever had to face. Through turning to God, I am strong enough to not only face those memories but also to overcome them. And I know that because I can do that, I can do anything.

Balance

— ◆ —

God guides me in living a balanced life.

A performer on a tightrope high above the circus crowd knows the importance of balance in helping him attain his goal—safely reaching the end of the rope on the other side.

Balance in my own life is just as important, for it enables me to keep things in perspective and then follow God's direction to a rich and satisfying life.

Physically, I remain balanced when I get plenty of sleep, eat the right foods, and give my body the exercise it needs to remain healthy and strong.

Mentally, I have the understanding I need from the light of God within. God created me, so I am a creation of wisdom and understanding.

Spiritually, I am nourished by my times in prayer with God. Any time is the right time to focus my attention on God and let God guide me in living a balanced life that is a joy to experience.

> "In him all things in heaven and on earth were created,
> things visible and invisible, whether thrones
> or dominions or rulers or powers."
> —Colossians 1:16

Restored

——◆——

*I am continually restored
by the life of God!*

I am a creation of divine design! How good I feel in just speaking this truth. I feel even better when I recognize that my true identity is an eternal spiritual being that is within my physical body.

The very spirit of God sustains and restores me. The light of life is aglow within me, renewing every cell and fiber of my being. The more I claim my true identity of a spiritual being, the more I am renewed in mind and body.

Alive with the life of God, I am in a constant state of renewal. My heart beats in a strong and steady rhythm of life. The birth of new cells takes place according to divine order.

Moment by moment, I am restored and healed, renewed and revitalized.

"Restore us to yourself, O Lord,
that we may be restored; renew our days as of old."
—Lamentations 5:21

Blessing of Forgiveness

——— ◆ ———

*Forgiveness is a blessing I can give
to myself and to others.*

At times I may find it is easier to forgive others than it is to forgive myself. This may be because I have recycled my past mistakes by replaying them time and time again in my mind.

I can end this unproductive cycle by remembering that I am a student of life—always learning and gathering wisdom from situations as they occur. Then I forgive myself. I acknowledge the achievements I have made and know that I will accomplish even more in the future!

I forgive myself! Affirming these words releases me from burdens of the past. I am free from former limitations because I have treated myself with the same love and respect that I have shown to others by forgiving them. What a blessing forgiveness is, and how much healthier I am when I experience the cleansing that forgiveness brings!

> "Create in me a clean heart, O God,
> and put a new and right spirit within me."
> —Psalms 51:10

Faith in God

—◆—

God is life and healing,
wisdom and love.

I let a prayer of faith rise up from within me and vibrate a message of life and healing throughout my body:

"God, I have faith in You. Your spirit of life within me is healing me now! Every cell of my body is expressing life.

"God, I have faith in You. With Your wisdom directing my decisions, I am a voice of compassion and thoughtfulness in my home, workplace, and community.

"God, I have faith in You. Because I am made in Your image, God, I believe in myself. I have faith that whenever I am totally aware of You and letting Your will be done, You are expressing life, love, and wisdom through me.

"God, I have faith in You, and I feel the assurance of Your faith in me as life and healing, wisdom and love."

"Blessed are those who trust in the Lord."
—Jeremiah 17:7

Healthy Living

—◆—

*My prayer breaks are part of my schedule
for healthy living.*

My schedule may seem hectic at times, but I can always find time for a prayer break—a quiet moment when I break away from physical and mental activity to enter into a peaceful time of prayer.

Even if I have only 5 or 10 minutes, I can move away from the hustle and bustle of the day to regain my composure and my stamina. Settling into a comfortable chair, I close my eyes and turn my thoughts inward to the presence of God.

In silence, I rest in God's presence. My mind is at ease, and my thoughts are positive. I have taken time to rest, and in this time I have gotten in touch with an inner peace that I can now apply to daily living.

Leaving my time of silence, I feel invigorated and renewed. As I continue with my day, I am amazed at how much better I feel—physically and emotionally— from a few moments of sacred communication with God.

"Your steadfast love, O Lord, extends to the heavens."
—Psalms 36:5

Making Progress

——◆——

God is my strength and comfort.
I am renewed in body and spirit.

Massage, exercise, heat, and water therapy can be aids to the natural healing process of the body. So if I am undergoing rehabilitation or a loved one is, I envision the good results taking place even before the evidence is apparent. My positive attitude encourages us throughout the treatment.

Although physical therapy may be uncomfortable at times, I know that progress is being made every day. Weakened muscles are once more being put to use and strengthened.

Throughout any therapy, I lean on God for support and comfort. While doing my rehabilitation exercises or while encouraging my loved ones to continue theirs, I keep my mind focused on the strength and energy we draw from God's presence. God in me and my loved ones is power and perseverance. We are on our way to a complete recovery.

"Paul, looking at him intently and seeing that he had faith
to be healed, said in a loud voice, 'Stand upright
on your feet.' And the man sprang up and began to walk."
—Acts 14:9

God Bless Health Care Workers

——◆——

*Health care workers are shining lights
of compassion and understanding.*

Today in my prayers, I bless the health care workers of the world. Their dedication to serving others is a commitment to helping people regain their health and even to experience greater health than they have ever before known.

If a loved one or I need medical attention, I feel relief in knowing that there are people who serve in health care fields who can give us the attention we need. There is something I can do for them in return; I remember them in my prayers:

"God, thank You for health care workers and their loving commitment to enhancing the lives of others. Surely their strength of spirit comes from You, for it expresses a sacred dedication to others. I pray that these caregivers receive blessings in return for all the blessings they have given. Most important, may they always know Your love and peace in their lives."

**"Therefore, my beloved, be steadfast, immovable, always excelling in the work of the Lord, because you know that in the Lord your labor is not in vain."
—1 Corinthians 15:58**

Today's Message:

Intuition

———— ◆ ————

Intuition is the wisdom of my heart
revealing the wisdom of God to me.

In praying about a question that is on my heart and
mind, how do I know that the answer I receive is from
God? I know because divine intuition, a wisdom of the
heart, connects me with the wisdom of God.

Intuition is an inner knowing, a personal message
of guidance that God gives to me so that I have the
understanding I need to work through the most
complicated situations life can offer. I know what to
say and do and I also know what to refrain from saying
and doing.

The wisdom of my heart reveals guidance from God.
Intuition, an inner urging, awakens me to a world of
possibilities and reminds me that God and I are in
charge of my life.

"You have stripped off the old self with its practices
and have clothed yourselves with the new self,
which is being renewed in knowledge according
to the image of its creator."
—Colossians 3:9–10

Meditation

———◆———

"Forgive and console him, so that he may not be overwhelmed by excessive sorrow. . . . I urge you to reaffirm your love for him."
—2 Corinthians 2:7–8

I do not doubt the power of love to restore and enhance my relationships. My part in this healing, restoring process is to be willing to open my heart in prayer to the love of God, which encourages me to love.

In prayer, I think of the people in my life. Out of one moment of anger, a lifetime of hurt can be caused. So I forgive them for things they may have done or said that caused me pain, or what they have not done or said that hurt me.

Next I send my loving thoughts to them and then envision them aglow with God's love. I visualize love being returned to and accepted by me. Then I relax and let love do its perfect work.

Whether the persons involved realize it or not, there can no longer be any animosity between them and me, because the transforming power of God has opened the way of love for us.

Prayer

——◆——

*"In your presence there is fullness of joy;
in your right hand are pleasures forevermore."*
—Psalms 16:11

God, I thought I knew what joy was until I gave up every thought of unworthiness and let You bring my awareness to my own sacredness.

When life seems to be pressing in on me, Your presence surrounds me and comforts me. O God, I feel so honored to know that the joy of Your spirit within me is living through me as vitality and healing, as compassion and reverence for all people, for all life.

The joy of Your spirit is a gladness of the soul that moves throughout my mind and body in wave after wave. I have an energy I never before realized was possible for me. I feel a kinship with others that strengthens all of my relationships.

God, I feel the joy of knowing Your presence right now!

Listen, Beloved

—◆—

Beloved,

You were created from My love. Because I love you, you will find that whenever you have a need—whether for healing, prosperity, or peace of mind—you will find the answers you seek by turning to Me.

You turn to the source of life by turning to Me. You turn to the source of love by turning to Me. You turn to the source of unlimited life and wholeness by turning to Me.

Love heals all, and your faith will guide you in being healthy and fulfilled. As you think of what you may need, see yourself as you were created to be—a being of health and wholeness.

You are a living miracle of muscle, tissue, and cells infused with divine love. All the care I have given to creating you is not by chance, for I created You from love and to be love.

"Every day I will bless you."
—Psalms 145:2

DAILY WORD FOR HEALING

God's Tender Care

———◆———

*I pray knowing that God is tenderly caring
for my loved ones.*

Although I may not be able to reach out to hug my
loved ones physically, I can reach out to embrace them
spiritually when I enfold them in a golden light of
prayer:

"God, as I pray for my loved ones, I bless them and I
also bless myself. As I whisper their names to You, I feel
waves of peace moving throughout my body. You are
there with them, and I pray that they are aware of Your
presence and follow Your guidance.

"Each thought I think about them and each prayer
I say silently or aloud supports them in fulfilling a life
of health, peace, love, and prosperity. Just as surely as
You are listening to me now, God, You are also listening
to them.

"There is no limit to Your love and caring—for my
loved ones and for me. Thank You, God, for loving us
and for caring for us so tenderly."

**"Finally, all of you, have unity of spirit, sympathy,
love for one another, a tender heart, and a humble mind."**
—1 Peter 3:8

Fresh Start

—— ◆ ——

*Today is the first day of a new start
in life for me.*

No matter what happened yesterday or last week or last year, today is a fresh start for me. I declare and believe that today is a new beginning for me.

Because I am embarking on a new adventure in life, I put aside regrets about what I did or did not do in the past. I am alive and living for the joy and wonder of today.

There will never again be a time when I can experience what this moment holds, so I open my mind and heart to the wondrous blessings that are awaiting my discovery.

God created me to live a life of wonder, so right now—this first day of my new start in life—is the perfect time for me to live as God created me to live. I am healthy, whole, and free.

"I told them that the hand of my God had been gracious
upon me, and also the words that the king had spoken
to me. Then they said, 'Let us start building!'
So they committed themselves to the common good."
—Nehemiah 2:18

God Takes No Time Off

——◆——

God is constantly blessing me—
day and night.

The presence of God is always active, for God takes no time off. God blesses me all during the day and night.

God's love for me is so great that I am surrounded by and enfolded in God's presence, which means that I am continually being renewed and restored. And because I am aware of God, I bring a sacred touch to everything that I think, say, or do.

I see the life of God reflected back to me as I look in the mirror, for I am an expression of God! I see God's love for me in a body that gives me form and substance. I have a mind that takes me beyond the realm of probability to the reality of divine possibilities. God assures me that I am worthy of a full and satisfying life. I feel so blessed in knowing that I am God's beloved creation of life and love.

> "I saw the Lord always before me . . .
> therefore my heart was glad, and my tongue rejoiced."
> —Acts 2:25–26

My Soul Rejoices

—◆—

*My soul overflows
with rejoicing.*

What greater fulfillment could I have than to have a soul
that rejoices? And having spiritual awareness—an
awareness of the spirit of God within me and others—is
cause for my soul to rejoice.

When I am busy working, I work from the
understanding that the spirit of God within me is my
source of strength and wisdom. My soul rejoices when
I know that whatever I do somehow touches the lives
of other people and blesses them.

My heart is filled with the gladness of tender
moments with family and friends. These special times
with longtime friends and new acquaintances enrich
my life.

My heart is filled with gladness and my soul
overflows with rejoicing because I am aware of God
within me, within others, and within the world.

**"Therefore my heart is glad,
and my soul rejoices."
—Psalms 16:9**

Thank You, God!

———◆———

Thank You, God, for working wonders through me and for healing all that needs to be healed!

If I let my human nature have absolute control of my thoughts, I may be too specific in my requests to God. Then I limit the outcomes and events to the way I would like them to happen.

Yet when I let my spiritual nature inspire me, I understand that there is no limit to how God blesses me. Life is a divine appointment. God has a plan for me, and through that plan God is working wonders through me, healing all that needs to be healed.

I do not lose hope when I am physically challenged. I know that the spirit of God lives within me and is able to heal and restore me. If a relationship between a loved one and me needs to be healed, I call on the spirit of God within us to unite us in love and understanding.

I thank God for an atmosphere of healing that works wonders through me and others.

"Wonderful are your works."
—Psalms 139:14

Gift of Today

———— ◆ ————

I live each day in the light and love of God.

I don't let myself become so busy trying to find all the blessings of life that each day holds that I let the blessings of this day slip away from me.

There is no way I can get back the time I waste with worry or fret. So I live each day to the fullest and enjoy each moment for the tremendous opportunity that it is. Whether I am involved in some demanding project or in quiet times of thought and reflection, I am in the presence of God. What greater blessing could I ask to receive than to be fully aware of God?

Yes, I can be and am blessed throughout the day with an abundance of blessings, but the greatest gift of all is the day itself—a day in which I can live and breathe and be joyous in the love of God.

My days are full of prosperity, for I am living in the light and love of God.

"And God is able to provide you with every blessing
in abundance, so that by always having enough
of everything, you may share abundantly in
every good work."
—2 Corinthians 9:8

Source of Life

—◆—

*I am alive
with the life of God!*

I have tremendous love and appreciation for my parents and grandparents. Yet I know that the source of the life that has come down through generations from the beginning of time and is now living out through me is from God.

Because God is the source of my life, I do not inherit sickness or disease. Even though one or both of my parents experienced some disorder, I dissolve any tendency to believe that I will also. I affirm: *The life living out through me is from God. I am a whole and healthy being of God's creation.*

My life-affirming words and thoughts give a boost to my own well-being. God's spirit is living in and through me as vitality and wisdom. I know and affirm this truth with every thought I think and every word I speak. I am alive with the life of God.

> "For the bread of God is that which comes down
> from heaven and gives life to the world."
> —John 6:33

TODAY'S MESSAGE:
Body and Soul

—◆—

I eat to nourish my body;
I pray to nourish my soul.

I thank God that I am able to enjoy the flavor and texture of the food I eat. As much as I enjoy eating, I know that there is something much more important in eating than simple enjoyment.

I eat to live—a healthy life. When I eat, I select food that nourishes my body. This is something important I can do for myself, and it is something I can do to honor the creation of God that I am.

I remember to feed my body and also feed my soul. Fresh, healthy food blesses my body with physical energy. Prayer blesses my soul with spiritual energy. The more I pray, the more I am blessed, for as I experience the presence of God, I am strengthened, calmed, and inspired.

Nourished body and soul, I am truly alive and living life fully. Knowing that I am a whole and holy being, I do more than cope with life; I enjoy life!

> "He rained down on them manna to eat,
> and gave them the grain of heaven."
> —Psalms 78:24

Meditation

—◆—

"The Lord does not see as mortals see;
they look on the outward appearance,
but the Lord looks on the heart."
—1 Samuel 16:7

I move away from focusing on what is happening
to me and around me to a few moments of
considering what is happening within me, at the
depths of my heart and soul.

When I look within in a time of prayer and
meditation, this is what I perceive: The spirit of God
is there sustaining and nourishing me. I behold the
beauty and majesty of a spiritual being—the true
me that rises above everyday concerns.

This is how it feels to know that I am a
beloved child of God. I know that there is so much
more to me than just my mind and my body. I am
a unique and awe-inspiring creation of the Creator
of all life—a being of beauty and light that reflects
the spirit of God back into the world.

Yes, looking within is a sacred activity that
reveals my true identity. I bask in the glow of this
divine revelation.

Prayer

—◆—

*"The fruit of the Spirit is love, joy, peace,
patience, kindness, generosity, faithfulness,
gentleness, and self-control."*
—*Galatians 5:22*

God, the joy within my soul is the gladness of the
spiritual being that I am. Even when I am going
through a difficult time, joy is within me because
Your spirit is within me. Thank You, God, for joy.

The joy of Your spirit within is a faithful source
of assurance for me. Like a tinkling bell, inner joy
reminds me of the constant stirring of life and hope
within me. It leads me through the valleys of life's
experiences and up onto the mountaintop of a
bright, new day.

Thank You, God, for planting the seed of joy
within me. I have nurtured that seed with my
awareness so I now recognize it as the fruit of Your
spirit within me. Oh, what an experience it is to
know and feel the joy of Your ever-constant
presence!

Listen, Beloved

—◆—

Beloved,

There is no blessing that I would withhold from you, for you are My creation, and I love you. I have created you for life, so live your life with the assurance that you are worthy of every blessing. Never worry about earning My love, for it is My gift to you.

Live well, My beloved, and face challenges with courage. You will never let mistakes bring you down, because going through a challenging time brings out strength you never before realized you had.

Allow yourself to both give and receive love. When others disappoint you, know that you are loved by Me—eternally.

You are My creation of life and love. In all the world there is no other like you, and you have a special purpose in life: to be an individual expression of My life and love in all that you do.

"Everything created by God is good."
—1 Timothy 4:4

DAILY WORD FOR HEALING

Gentle Heart

——◆——

*I have a gentle heart
that is a radiating center of peace.*

Do I ever feel stressed because of what is happening to me and around me? Then I accept the invitation that Jesus gave to all who long for peace of mind: "Take my yoke upon you, and learn from me; for I am gentle and humble in heart, and you will find rest for your souls" (Matthew 11:29).

The gentleness I bring to any situation helps dissipate any anxiety or stress I am feeling and also helps put others in my workplace or home at ease. Because I am calm, I have a clear understanding of what is mine to do and the best way to go about doing it.

Having a gentle heart is having a reverence for life and everyone and everything in life. I give thanks for a gentle heart, a heart that radiates a peacefulness that blesses me and those who share my life.

> "Take my yoke upon you, and learn
> from me; for I am gentle and humble in heart,
> and you will find rest for your souls."
> —Matthew 11:29

I Am Courageous

———◆———

*Because God is expressing life and power
through me, I am courageous.*

The greatest challenges in life seem to bring out
extraordinary courage in ordinary people.

I believe this is true for me in critical times, for I do
rely on the presence of God in me and in the other
people involved in the situation. In surrendering all to
God, I realize I have courage I never before dreamed
was possible for me.

What a lift to my spirits it is to know that God and I
are working through a challenge or a crisis. Such a
positive way of praying and thinking leads me in taking
effective actions. I can be compassionate and caring
toward others and at the same time be committed to
doing whatever is for the good of all.

My courage rises from my belief in the miracle-
working power of God and from my belief that God is
expressing life and power through me.

> "Surely God is my salvation;
> I will trust, and will not be afraid."
> —Isaiah 12:2

Lifted Up

— ◆ —

*The spirit of God shines from my soul, uplifting me
and brightening my day.*

To be lifted up in spirit is to be renewed with life.
Uplifted in spirit, I know what the sunflower must
experience as its bowed head is brought upright by the
warmth and energy of the sun.

Yet the light that uplifts me comes from within, from
the spirit of God that is always shining brightly within
my soul. Whenever I am feeling down, I call on my
faith to open the door to my soul and let the light of
God's presence shine out through me.

Uplifted in spirit, I am transformed physically.
Any tension I once felt melts away, leaving me
completely relaxed and at ease. I feel truly alive as I
breathe deeply and fill my lungs with oxygen-rich air.
I am lifted up so that I convey a loving, peaceful
approach in life that helps to brighten my day and the
day of those around me.

> "Jesus took him by the hand and lifted him up,
> and he was able to stand."
> —Mark 9:27

Right Outcome

———◆———

I expect right outcomes in all matters,
for God is continually blessing me.

Each day I am learning more about God and the wonder
of God's creativity.

I thank God for being patient with me even when I
am being impatient with God. My impatience comes
about when what I think is the right outcome does not
happen quickly enough. But the right outcome does
occur in divine order, and I realize that God is blessing
me beyond what I ever imagined could be.

I have hopes and dreams, but I know that God will
bless me with so much more than I can envision. The
horizon of my life is bright with blessings. I am thankful
that God never places any limitations or conditions on
loving me. God's unconditional love inspires me to
grow beyond my own limited thinking, and I expect to
be blessed.

> "Blessed be the Lord, for he has wondrously
> shown his steadfast love to me."
> —Psalms 31:21

Life of God

——◆——

*I am a living expression of the life
of God within me.*

It is amazing how the healing life of God within me
quickly responds to a cut on my finger. I am watching
the life of God within me come forward to heal an
injury as day by day the cut fades and a complete
healing takes place.

Day by day I give thanks that God created me to
heal. The cells of my body have an intelligence that
responds immediately to heal and repair an injury. I am
healed!

I am able to heal because I have been blessed with an
amazing body—a temple of God through which divine
life is expressed continually. And though I may not look
the same or perform at the same level as others, I am
blessed with life. So I bless my body each day by giving
thanks that through it, I express the life and healing of
God's spirit within.

> "The prayer of the righteous
> is powerful and effective."
> —James 5:16

Rose-Colored Day

——◆——

This is a rose-colored day
that is full of possibilities.

Am I a person who is so optimistic that I look at the
world through rose-colored glasses—glasses that make
people and situations seem better than they may appear
to be? Well, realizing that I live in a world that God
created, I am just naturally optimistic.

When I look ahead to my day, to my future, I see all
from an optimistic point of view—past current
challenges to divine results. By considering myself, all
other people, and all situations through the love of God
that I feel, I see the unlimited possibilities and endless
probabilities that are before me.

I see the glory of God in everyday life. When I meet
new people, I remember that the divine spark of life is
within them, just as it is within me. My rose-colored
glasses represent a soul filled with faith, a heart filled
with love, and a person willing to see the glory of God
in everyone and everywhere.

> **"The measure you give will be**
> **the measure you get back."**
> **—Luke 6:38**

Center of Love

———◆———

*My heart is a center
of love and peace.*

What a miracle of life God has created in my heart! As
my heart beats in a steady rhythm and pumps life-
renewing blood throughout my body, it sustains and
nourishes the cells and organs of my body. Then every
cell, organ, and function works in harmony to support
my whole body.

My heart is also a center of spiritual activity—a
symbol for how I experience God's love and express
God's love. Every beat of my heart is a reminder of the
love of God for me and keeps a virtual flow of life
coursing throughout my body. I give thanks for a heart
that supplies me with nourishment that energizes me.
I am vitally alive as a true expression of the spirit of God
within.

I have love to spare so I share it with others,
connecting with them in a circle of love that promotes
harmony and peace.

> "If we love one another, God lives in us,
> and his love is perfected in us."
> —1 John 4:12

God Is My All

———◆———

God is my all.

God is the spirit of life within me—life that provides me with all the energy and strength I will ever need to live an active and fulfilling life.

God is the love I feel when I see a friend or neighbor smile, the comfort I receive from a thoughtful word or a tender touch.

God is the light that shines on me day after day and the wisdom I need to make decisions.

God is the inspiration that rises within me when others say there is no hope. I will not despair, for God, the creator of all hope, is with me.

God is the beginning and the end, the source of all that ever was, is, or will be. God's eternal gift to me is a never-ending flow of all that I could ever want or desire.

God is my all.

> "The Lord your God is indeed God
> in heaven above and on earth below."
> —Joshua 2:11

THE MIRACLE OF AMANDA
BY SCOTT NEIL MACLELLAN

A manda is our miracle child. When she was just 2 days old, she developed a high fever and my wife, Deborah, and I rushed her to the emergency room at the hospital. For a week, the doctors tried but never discovered what had caused the fever.

That visit to the hospital became the first of many in the first 2 years of Amanda's life. She would have high fevers with an ear infection, a cold, or the flu. Still, the doctors didn't know why she was so sick so often.

When she was about 2 years old, we moved from Atlanta to Chicago. Because one of Amanda's symptoms was a severe rash, we took her to a new dermatologist in Chicago.

Finally, Amanda's condition was diagnosed as Langerhan's cell histiocytosis, a rare disease. A specialist found that the rash was not only on her skin and in her ears, but that it had invaded her liver as well. Because the condition of her liver had advanced to a serious stage, she was started on chemotherapy. Her liver never recovered, and she eventually needed a liver transplant.

Time was running out for Amanda, and she was on a long list of people waiting for a liver donor. A new liver transplant procedure had been pioneered at the University of Chicago Medical Center, however, and Amanda was enrolled. Through this program, I was able to donate part of my liver to Amanda.

Unfortunately, the drugs that were used to keep Amanda's new liver from being rejected suppressed her immune system. At age 4, she developed lymphoma—with a tumor the size of a grapefruit growing inside her chest. After surgery and 6 months of chemotherapy, the tumor had shrunk to the size of a quarter. But because the tumor was still there, she continued on chemotherapy for a year.

At the end of the year, we received devastating news: The cancer had returned and was growing around and into her heart. Even with a new round of chemo, the doctors held little hope for Amanda.

The hospital was 2 hours away from home. And even though I had a full-time job and we had another daughter, Sarah, at home, either Deborah or I was always with Amanda.

Such challenges can rip a family apart, but Sarah was a wonderful inspiration for Deborah and me. She was such a joy to come home to because she would share her excitement about the smallest things in life. She would bring us back immediately to what we were called to do—to have joy and wonder about everything in life. I told her: "Sarah, you are what I think Christ asks all of us to be. You have such a wonderful, childlike spirit."

I went through the cycle of denial, anger, and bitterness. It was faith that got Deborah and me through some very grim times. Despite the fact that the doctors thought Amanda could not live much longer, Deborah and I held on to our faith. Life was in no way perfect for us as individuals or as a family, but when we were able to accept that it didn't have to be perfect, Amanda started getting better.

After several more years of chemo, Amanda is doing well. She shows no signs of cancer. We are living from the faith that the cancer is gone forever. Her most lingering challenge is a hearing impairment. One of her eardrums had to be reconstructed. Yet if you were to see her today, you would never guess what she has been through. She goes to school and has even qualified for state gymnastics. She is an active, normal child.

Throughout Amanda's long road to healing, journaling was a form of prayer for me. I believe God often spoke to me through my own writing. As I journaled, I discovered the answers I needed to be able to help Amanda, the rest of our family, and myself.

I wrote the book *Amanda's Gift* from that journaling. I think one of the greatest lessons I learned was acceptance as a form of surrender to God. I accepted everything and had faith that God would bring about a miracle. I stopped fighting the disease that threatened to take Amanda and constantly seemed to overwhelm my whole family. Then I was able to find some measure of hope and joy every day.

When I did let go and let God, as I had so often read about in *Daily Word*, I stopped needing to know what the final solution would be. I surrendered to God's will, and I believe that surrender led to a miracle for Amanda and for us all.

ABOUT THE
FEATURED AUTHORS

Bonnie St. John Deane, at 16, was a young girl with one leg and big dreams. Within 5 years, she became an Olympic ski medalist, a Harvard honors graduate, and a Rhodes scholar. Bonnie has worked in the financial market on Wall Street as well as in Europe and Asia and as an award-winning sales representative for IBM. A writer, speaker, and president of SJD&Co., she also serves as a national spokesperson for Disabled Sports/USA. Bonnie has been featured by NBC Nightly News as one of the five most inspiring women in the nation. She currently resides in San Diego with her daughter and husband.

Mick Dustin, an ordained Unity minister, has served as senior minister of Unity Church of Pasadena in Texas; the director of the Unity Village Chapel Counseling and Resource Center at Unity School of Christianity; and director of Education for the Association of Unity Churches. Mick's wife, Christine, serves as the Retreat Ministries director at Unity School of Christianity.

Bill Goss, a highly sought-after professional speaker, has worked for a sanitation department, been a Golden Gloves boxer, and become an underwater explosives expert. After college he became a Navy pilot and spent time on an aircraft carrier and a nuclear submarine. His inspiring struggle to survive cave-ins, car and plane crashes, cancer, and more is recounted in his book, *The Luckiest Unlucky Man Alive*.

Karolyn (Zuzu) Grimes is probably best known for her famous line, "Every time a bell rings, an angel gets his wings." Since the age of 4, Karolyn has appeared in 16 movies including *The Bishop's Wife*, *Hans Christian Andersen*, and *It's a Wonderful Life*. She is sought after as a speaker and provides an extensive Web site and newsletter for The Zuzu Fan Society.

Julie Hanna, a graduate of Denison University in Ohio, works for the Columbus Zoo in Ohio as well as speaks on behalf of the Leukemia Society. Her father, "Jungle" Jack Hanna, is director emeritus of the Columbus Zoo and host of the television series *Jack Hanna's Animal Adventures*.

Mary L. Kupferle has been an ordained Unity minister since 1959. She is a longtime friend and member of the Unity and *Daily Word* family. Now semi-retired, Mary remains active in the Unity movement through her inspirational writings. She is a channel through whom millions of people are blessed and uplifted.

Scott Neil MacLellan, author of *Amanda's Gift*, has been quoted in several articles and periodicals on health, wellness, and business. He is also a published poet and is working on his second book. Scott is the president of a large, Atlanta-based business and resides in Roswell, Georgia, with his wife, Deborah, and daughters, Sarah and Amanda.

Larry Moore is an award-winning primary news anchor for KMBC-TV and cohost of the annual Variety Club Telethon in Kansas City, Missouri. He has received numerous honors for his community work with children, including being awarded the 1989 Good Shepherd Award and the Stephen K. Douglas

Outstanding Volunteer Award by the Dream Factory. Larry and his wife, Ruth, are the parents of five children.

Kathy Nelson, an ordained Unity minister, is currently serving at the Christ Unity Church in Charlotte, North Carolina. She attended Drury College in Springfield, Missouri, and the University of California, Irvine. She and her husband, David, have three children and seven grandchildren.

Mel Richardson, M.D., is medical director and chief of staff of the Indian River Memorial Hospital Ambulatory Surgery Center. He is associated with the American Society of Anesthesiologists, the Society of Ambulatory Anesthesiologists, and the American Medical Association.

Dennis Young is an ordained Unity minister. He is currently serving as associate minister at Unity Church of Christ in Houston and lives with his wife, Jane, a kindergarten teacher, and their cat, Sammy.

ABOUT THE FEATURED AUTHORS